GR8NESS

CELEBRATING THE KENTUCKY WILDCATS' 8TH NATIONAL CHAMPIONSHIP

LEXINGTON HERALD-LEADER

Kentucky.com

Rufus Friday, Publisher
Peter Baniak, Editor
Gene Abell, Sports Editor
Mat Graf, Assistant Sports Editor
Rob Kandt, News Editor
Ron Garrison, Multimedia Editor
Sharon Ruble, Technology and Production Manager
Brian Simms, Design Director
Jerry Tipton, Reporter
John Clay, Columnist
Mark Story, Columnist
Charles Bertram, Chief Photographer
Mark Cornelison, Photographer
David Perry, Photographer
Pablo Alcalá, Photographer

KCI SPORTS PUBLISHING

Peter J. Clark, Publisher
Molly Voorheis, Managing Editor
Nicky Brillowski, Book and Cover Design
Sam Schmidt, Advertising

ISBN: 978-0-9837337-5-1 (PB)
ISBN: 978-0-9837337-3-7 (HC)

Printed in the United States of America
KCI Sports Publishing 3340 Whiting Avenue, Suite 5 Stevens Point, WI 54481
Phone: 1-800-697-3756 Fax: 715-344-2668
www.kcisports.com

CONTENTS

FOREWORD

For fans of Kentucky basketball, 14 years was like an eternity.

The program with the most wins in the history of college basketball hadn't cut down the nets in the NCAA Tournament since 1998, when it capped a run that saw it go to the finals three straight times (also winning it all in 1996).

More than a decade later, Kentucky's 2010-11 season ended with a trip to the Final Four, and a loss to UConn one game before the tournament finals. Fans in Big Blue Nation were happy to be back in the big dance, but the early exit from the Final Four left them wanting even more.

What they really wanted coming into the 2011-12 season was an eighth championship banner to hang in Rupp Arena in downtown Lexington. And many thought UK had finally found the right combination to capture another crown.

The team came into the season with the most highly-touted freshman class in college basketball, a trademark of Coach John Calipari in the three seasons since he took over the program. Add to the mix three key returning players from the 2011 Final Four team in Terrence Jones, Doron Lamb and Kentuckian Darius Miller. Then, stir in Coach Cal himself, the master-recruiter, coach and social media hype-builder.

The 2011-12 season lived up to fans' expectations from the moment the team took the stage at Big Blue Madness. The Wildcats roared through the season, won the SEC regular-season title with a 16-0 conference record and finished with an overall record of 38-2. Kentucky dominated its NCAA Tournament games, winning two key rivalry games against Indiana (avenging one of its two season losses) and against in-state rival Louisville in the Final Four.

When Kentucky defeated that other college basketball titan Kansas in the title game in Blue Orleans, it capped off a dream season for the team and its huge fan base, and added that coveted eighth national title to Kentucky basketball lore.

Along the way, the award-winning staff of the Lexington Herald-Leader and Kentucky.com chronicled Kentucky's title run. On these pages, you will find a selection of their most memorable work from a season Kentucky fans won't soon forget.■

- Peter Baniak, Editor,
  Lexington Herald-Leader

- Rufus Friday, Publisher,
  Lexington Herald-Leader

After defeating Kansas in the championship game, the Wildcats celebrated Kentucky's eighth national title.
Mark Cornelison | Lexington Herald-Leader

TEAGUE
25

BY: JERRY TIPTON

10 QUESTIONS FOR THE CATS

What does the lack of a "true" center mean for the dribble-drive offense, defensive sets and rebounding? Kentucky lacked a "true" center last season and advanced to the Final Four. So the lack of a "true" center is no serious handicap. Without such a player, a path can be more easily cleared for drives toward the basket, so any dribble-drive action can be enhanced by the absence of a lane-clogging post-up man. On defense, freshmen Anthony Davis and Michael Kidd-Gilchrist, plus others, will block shots. Denny Crum led Louisville to multiple Final Fours and won two national championships with "smaller" teams that fronted the post. Those Louisville teams are the example Kentucky might follow.

If Marquis Teague goes down, what does UK do for a point guard? To borrow a John Calipari term, there is no point guard with "demonstrated performance" on the roster. But, if form holds, Teague will be plenty good as the starter. But who takes over if Teague misses extended time because of injury? Foul trouble in a particular game can be handled. Players such as Darius Miller, Doron Lamb and Terrence Jones can be temporary fixes. Twany Beckham and Jarrod Polson could get UK through a stretch of minutes. Long term, UK needs Teague on the floor and steadily improving throughout the season like predecessors John Wall and Brandon Knight.

Freshmen Anthony Davis and Michael Kidd-Gilchrist talked during Big Blue Madness. *Mark Cornelison | Lexington Herald-Leader*

Is there anybody the Cats can't afford to lose? (Other than John Calipari, of course.) On UK's Media Day, Calipari likened this group to the Louisville teams of the 1970s and 1980s. Crum used interchangeable players whose versatility propelled the Cards to six Final Fours in a 15-year period. Aside from point guard, UK seems blessed with multiple options at the other four positions. But one player stands out in this cast ensemble. Jones did so many things well last season, as evidenced by 13 double-doubles, he won a media vote to be the Southeastern Conference's Player of the Year this season. His combination of size, productivity and experience make him first among equals.

Who will take the big shots late in games for this team? Last season Kentucky had an 8-8 record in games decided by

The UK team watched as the 2011 Final Four banner was hung during Big Blue Madness.
Mark Cornelison | Lexington Herald-Leader

seven or fewer points. That reflects the precarious nature of close games and, perhaps, UK's lack of a dominant low-post presence, which can ensure high-percentage shots and/or free throws at crunch time. The Cats could have several low-post options this season: lobs to Davis, hooks from Kyle Wiltjer, clever moves from Jones. But there's no Jared Sullinger in the bunch. If it comes down to perimeter shooting, UK is well armed. Doron Lamb (48.6 percent) and Darius Miller (44.3) finished 1-2 in three-point accuracy among SEC shooters last season.

Jones burst out of the starting gate last year, much of it against lesser competition, semi-disappeared for much of the season just aimlessly wandering the perimeter and then seemed to make a comeback late. What can be expected of him this year? Jones did not simply feast on weaker competition. His double-doubles included 16 points and 17 rebounds against Washington, 27 points and 17 rebounds against Notre Dame and 11 points and 15 rebounds against UConn in the Final Four. These are monstrous numbers for a freshman. During the pre-season, Calipari has noted Jones' greater level of fitness and keener sense of purpose as a sophomore. This season, he's moved better and shown a take-charge attitude on the court. Calipari says Jones wants to be a solid lottery pick. Few would argue about that goal being achievable.

How long can Calipari keep up the run of No. 1 recruiting classes? During his first state-of-the-program Big Blue Madness address, Calipari set a goal of having every prospect in the country wanting to play for Kentucky. Even with the NCAA and its 13-player limit on scholarships, Calipari has seemingly come close enough to achieving that goal. Clearly, the one-and-done phenomenon helps by keeping a revolving door spinning. Each freshman departure opens up another opportunity for a prospect eyeing a fast track to the NBA. Of course, No. 1 recruiting classes are not a be-all, end-all — as Butler (2010 and 2011) and Virginia Commonwealth (2011) showed in recent Final Four runs.

UK players scrimmaged during Big Blue Madness in Rupp Arena. *Mark Cornelison | Lexington Herald-Leader*

Will Twany Beckham be of much help after he becomes eligible at the end of the fall semester? Beckham — surprise — is the oldest UK player. He turns 23 on Nov. 14. So he presumably brings a level of maturity that can help a team dependent on contributions from multiple freshmen. After finishing his high school career at Ballard in 2007, Beckham played a season at prep school. He then spent three seasons on the Mississippi State team, seeing playing time in SEC and NCAA Tournaments. He sat out 2009-10 because of hip surgery. Mississippi State Coach Rick Stansbury, who needed point guard help, lamented the absence. Given UK's need for a backup point guard, Beckham surely will get a chance to contribute

What will be UK's record against the four big-name, non-conference opponents: Kansas, North Carolina, Indiana and Louisville? A No. 2 pre-season ranking would represent being underrated should Kentucky sweep these four games. In the coaches' pre-season poll, North Carolina (No. 1), Louisville (No. 8) and Kansas (No. 13) were in the top 15. It can't hurt that North Carolina and Louisville will play UK in Rupp Arena. Kansas, the pre-season pick to win the Big 12, will be a difficult opponent on a neutral court in the second game of the season. The guess here is that Kentucky loses to Kansas and North Carolina, but beats Indiana and Louisville.

Will Darius Miller become more assertive? Hopefully so, if for no other reason than to spare readers the chore of slogging through another story about whether Miller will be more assertive. As Calipari likes to point out, Miller was voted Most Valuable Player of the 2011 SEC Tournament. He averaged 13.3 points and 5.6 rebounds. So it's not like he's been invisible. But those numbers slipped to 6.3 points and 3.0 rebounds in UK's last four NCAA Tournament games. He made eight of 27 shots in that span. As a senior, it's now or never for Miller. He led Mason County to the state

championship as a senior, so history suggests this will be Miller's time.

How will this freshman class compare to the past two at UK? Finishing third in this race is no disgrace. We're talking the Three Tenors. The first freshman class produced two All-Americans — not "freshman All-Americans," but All-Americans — in John Wall and DeMarcus Cousins. The second advanced to the Final Four. Jon Hood said it well when asked to compare the freshman classes. "Play a round-robin tournament between those three freshman classes," he said. "That'd get more publicity than most NBA games. It'd get a ton more publicity than the Dominicans against the pro team guys."■

Left: Freshman Michael Kidd-Gilchrist at Big Blue Madness. *Mark Cornelison | Lexington Herald-Leader*

Bottom Left: Doron Lamb showed his "three goggles" as he was introduced during Big Blue Madness on Oct. 14. *Mark Cornelison | Lexington Herald-Leader*

Bottom Right: Senior guard Darius Miller greeted fans during Big Blue Madness. *Amy Wallot | Lexington Herald-Leader*

VS. KANSAS

WILDCATS 75
JAYHAWKS 65

MADISON SQUARE GARDEN **NOVEMBER 15, 2011**

BY: JERRY TIPTON REGULAR SEASON

GARDEN PARTY

Kentucky comes together and dominates Jayhawks in second half

As the song New York, New York commands, start spreading the news. Kentucky has another quality team in the national sense of the term.

After Duke Coach Mike Krzyzewski made history here Tuesday night, UK whipped No. 12 Kansas 75-65. Suffocating defense propelled the Cats to victory in the second game of the Champions Classic, a made-for-TV doubleheader featuring four of college basketball's top programs.

In the first game, Duke beat Michigan State to enable Krzyzewski to become the winningest coach in Division I history.

UK Coach John Calipari had said Monday that a close game might expose the precocious Cats.

A 13-2 run to open the second half postponed that concern for later this season. UK (2-0) broke from a 28-28 halftime tie to take its first double-digit lead inside the first five minutes after halftime. In that span, Kansas made only one of 10 shots en route to a 28.1-percent shooting half. Kentucky blocked five attempts.

Thereafter, Kansas did not get within single digits until the final 30 seconds.

"I thought our defense was half decent," said Calipari, who did not sound pleased with the game's ups (second half) and downs (first half). "It's nice to block shots."

Thomas Robinson, whom Kansas bills as a candidate for Big 12 Player of the Year, lost his composure with 6:11 left. In a rebound tug of war, he ran into Terrence Jones, who fell to the court. Then he stepped over the UK player.

Calipari came down from the other end of the court to play peacemaker, seemingly telling agitated freshman Michael Kidd-Gilchrist to calm down.

Above: Michael Kidd-Gilchrist got a pat on the head from Doron Lamb after he scored and drew a foul against Kansas. *Mark Cornelison | Lexington Herald-Leader*

Right: Anthony Davis dunked home two of his 14 points against Kansas in Madison Square Garden. *Mark Cornelison | Lexington Herald-Leader*

Doron Lamb led a balanced UK attack with 17 points. Jones added 15, while freshman Anthony Davis had 14. Marquis Teague and Kidd-Gilchrist added 12 each.

KENTUCKY
23
KANSAS

Kansas (1-1) got 22 points from guard Tyshawn Taylor. Robinson struggled to score 11 and grabbed 12 rebounds. The teams were tied at halftime 28-28. That marked something of a triumph for Kentucky, which trailed much of the half and by as much as seven.

"We don't believe we truly have to play together yet," Calipari said. "It's not talent that wins."

Perhaps a sign of dependence on freshmen, turnovers hurt UK. The Cats committed 12 first-half turnovers, six by freshman point guard Teague.

Michael Kidd-Gilchrist was restrained by teammates as he exchanged words with Kansas guard Tyshawn Taylor. *Mark Cornelison | Lexington Herald-Leader*

Teague's poor half began with the public address announcer mispronouncing his first name during introductions ("Mar-KEES," he said). Teague finished the half with no assists and the six turnovers, thereby contributing mightily to Kentucky's assist-to-turnover ratio of 4-12.

Three of Kentucky's turnovers came on its first eight trips downcourt. Neither team scored until Jones posted up for a heavily contested shot to put the Cats ahead 2-0 with 17:57 left.

"We're not a good team yet," Calipari said. "(The Cats) broke off every play. What I have to start doing, you break off a play, you're coming out. ... Everybody walked into that game today; they were going to do their own thing."

Kansas took the initiative thereafter, taking a 10-3 lead.

Kentucky inched ahead 11-10 on Kidd-Gilchrist's fast-break layup with 11:39 left.

Conner Teahan gave Kansas a much-needed boost with two three-pointers from the left corner. Neither was a surprise for a senior who made seven of 10 three-point shots during exhibition play and three of four in the opener against Towson.

Travis Releford's dunk — one of six for the Jayhawks in the half — put Kansas ahead 21-14 with 7:43 left.

Kentucky called time and went to Jones, who hadn't scored since the game's first basket. He responded with seven points down the stretch. His rainbow three-pointer with two minutes left tied it at 26.

With Davis dunking twice (his third and fourth jams of the game), UK took its largest lead early in the second half. A 34-30 UK lead prompted a Kansas timeout at the 18:13 mark.

That didn't slow down UK. After Kansas missed a forced shot, Jones sped to a fast-break dunk. A block of Robinson's post-up caused Teague to break into a wide smile and clap happily. After UK blocked Teahan's leaner, Teague had more reason to smile as he hit a three-pointer (his first basket) to put the Cats ahead 39-30.

That prompted another Kansas timeout with 17:15 left.

Kansas went scoreless on its next four possessions (including two UK blocks). A Davis tip-in made the lead 41-30, completing a 13-2 Kentucky run to open the second half.

Lamb, coming up big in his homecoming, made sure there was no Kansas rally. He made three three-pointers in barely two minutes. The third put Kentucky ahead 54-37 with 10:16 left.

When Darius Miller hit a three-pointer a moment later, filmmaker Spike Lee got up from his end-line seat and departed. No drama here.■

BOX SCORE

KENTUCKY

	TOT-FG	3-PT		REBOUNDS									
## Player Name	FG-FGA	FG-FGA	FT-FTA	OF	DE	TOT	PF	TP	A	TO	BLK	S	MIN
03 Jones, Terrence..... f	6-11	1-2	2-2	2	5	7	4	15	2	2	3	1	35
14 Kidd-Gilchrist, M... f	4-9	1-3	3-5	1	8	9	3	12	4	5	3	1	35
23 Davis, Anthony......c	6-8	0-1	2-6	1	5	6	4	14	0	3	7	2	33
20 Lamb, Doron.........g	4-8	3-5	6-8	2	2	4	2	17	1	1	0	1	34
25 Teague, Marquis.....g	4-9	1-1	3-7	0	2	2	4	12	3	6	0	0	33
01 Miller, Darius......	2-5	1-3	0-1	2	2	4	1	5	4	2	0	0	20
30 Vargas, Eloy........	0-1	0-0	0-0	0	2	2	1	0	0	0	0	0	7
33 Wiltjer, Kyle.......	0-0	0-0	0-0	0	0	0	1	0	0	0	0	0	3
TEAM...............													
Totals.............	26-51	7-15	16-29	8	26	34	20	75	14	19	13	5	200

TOTAL FG%	1st Half:	10-26 38.5%	2nd Half:	16-25 64.0%	Game:	51.0%	DEADB
3-Pt. FG%	1st Half:	1-6 16.7%	2nd Half:	6-9 66.7%	Game:	46.7%	REBS
F Throw %	1st Half:	7-12 58.3%	2nd Half:	9-17 52.9%	Game:	55.2%	5

KANSAS

	TOT-FG	3-PT		REBOUNDS									
## Player Name	FG-FGA	FG-FGA	FT-FTA	OF	DE	TOT	PF	TP	A	TO	BLK	S	MIN
00 Robinson, Thomas...f	5-12	0-0	1-2	3	9	12	5	11	1	2	1	0	27
24 Releford, Travis.... f	2-6	0-2	0-0	0	3	3	0	4	0	5	0	2	28
05 Withey, Jeff........ c	3-4	0-0	1-2	3	3	6	3	7	1	2	4	1	25
10 Taylor, Tyshawn..... g	3-13	1-2	15-17	0	1	1	3	22	2	0	0	2	33
15 Johnson, Elijah..... g	3-11	1-4	1-2	1	0	1	4	8	4	1	0	3	32
01 Tharpe, Naadir......	0-4	0-2	0-0	0	1	1	1	0	1	2	0	2	9
02 Teahan, Conner......	3-7	2-5	0-0	1	1	2	4	8	0	2	0	0	23
04 Wesley, Justin......	1-1	0-0	3-4	1	4	5	4	5	0	0	0	0	21
40 Young, Kevin........	0-1	0-0	0-0	1	1	2	1	0	0	0	0	0	2
TEAM...............				4	2	6							
Totals.............	20-59	4-15	21-27	14	25	39	25	65	9	14	5	10	200

TOTAL FG%	1st Half:	11-27 40.7%	2nd Half:	9-32 28.1%	Game:	33.9%	DEADB
3-Pt. FG%	1st Half:	3-8 37.5%	2nd Half:	1-7 14.3%	Game:	26.7%	REBS
F Throw %	1st Half:	3-6 50.0%	2nd Half:	18-21 85.7%	Game:	77.8%	5

Officials: Mark Whitehead, Doug Shows, Antinio Petty

Technical fouls: Kentucky — None. Kansas — None.

Attendance: 19,979

Score by Periods	1st	2nd	Total
Kentucky	28	47	75
Kansas	28	37	65

Above: Darius Miller put in a shot over Kansas center Jeff Withey. Kentucky defeated Kansas 75-65 in the State Farm Champions Classic at Madison Square Garden.
Mark Cornelison | Lexington Herald-Leader

Left: Anthony Davis scored 14 points against Kansas during the State Farm Champions Classic in New York City.
Mark Cornelison | Lexington Herald-Leader

VS. ST. JOHN'S

WILDCATS 81
RED STORM 59

RUPP ARENA **DECEMBER 1, 2011**

BY: JERRY TIPTON REGULAR SEASON

BLOCK AND BLUE

Kentucky's sluggish offense offset by tight defense, Davis' swatting spree

Freshman Anthony Davis flirted with the second triple-double in Kentucky basketball history as the Cats smo Freshman Anthony Davis flirted with the second triple-double in Kentucky basketball history as the Cats smothered St. John's 81-59 Thursday night in Rupp Arena.

Davis set career highs with 15 rebounds and eight blocks while also scoring 15 points. Before exiting with 4:44 left, he appeared to block a ninth shot, which would have equaled a UK individual record (shared by Andre Riddick and Sam Bowie). But a foul call nullified the block.

"Even Coach Cal said that wasn't a foul," Davis said.

Davis' blocks fueled a defense that made St. John's live up to its billing as the nation's youngest team.

"Without him, we probably lose the game," UK Coach John Calipari said. "He changed everything about the game."

All the defense, which included a school-record 18 blocks, obscured Kentucky's continuing evolution on offense. Before the game, Calipari said the Cats were not yet "in sync" offensively. He said much the same after the game.

"We were just inept offensively," Calipari said.

Terrence Jones, who equaled a career-high of four blocks while scoring a game-high 26 points, explained how Kentucky could be so dominant defensively and struggle on offense.

"I feel it's easier," he said of defense. "You can help. We're long. It takes less thinking."

Davis' replacement, Eloy Vargas, got the record-breaking block with about two minutes left. That broke the previous mark of 17 blocks against Morehead State on Nov. 20, 1997.

Marquis Teague flew toward the basket past Sir'Dominic Pointer in the first half. *Pablo Alcalá | Lexington Herald-Leader*

For Davis, the defense and shot-blocking is a matter of personal pride. When asked why he pays so much attention to defense, he credited an AAU coach.

"He told us, if (the opponent) gets in the lane, they're getting into your mom's kitchen," he said.

With less than five minutes remaining in the first half, St. John's had been guilty of as many 35-second shot clock violations (five) as it had scored baskets (five). No wonder Kentucky led at halftime.

UK rode defense to a 31-20 lead at intermission. The Cats blocked 10 shots and limited St. John's to 8-for-27 shooting.

Asked to comment on Davis' shot-blocking, St. John's assistant coach Mike Dunlap said, "Well, he has really long arms, and he's very good at it. We wish we had one of those."

The defense came in handy because Kentucky did not get the more efficient offense that Calipari sought. The Cats made only 11 of their first 29 shots, which helped explain why St. John's trailed by as few as eight points with less than three minutes left in the half.

Kentucky finished the half with a flourish. Leading 29-20, Marquis Teague stepped to the foul line with 5.9 seconds left. He missed the front end of a one-and-

Terrence Jones drove to the basket in the second half. *Pablo Alcalá | Lexington Herald-Leader* one, but Jones took the rebound in front of the rim and dunked it home. That set the halftime score and gave Jones, the only scorer in double figures at the break, 13 points.

Kentucky's stingy defense came without much contribution from Michal Kidd-Gilchrist. The high-energy freshman picked up his second foul at the 14:29 mark and had little to show in the first half (no points, three turnovers in 10 minutes).

Both teams lived down to their track records for slow starts. Kentucky made only two of its first 12 shots.

St. John's, which came into the game shooting 47 percent (against a schedule ranked 230th toughest in the nation by Collegerpi.com) made five of its first 20 shots.

Worse, the Red Storm did not get off a shot on five possessions.

St. John's two leading scorers — Nurideen Lindsey and D'Angelo Harrison — missed all seven of their first-half shots.

Except for UK's increased efficiency, nothing changed in the second half.

A good start to the half got even better when Davis swatted away a driving shot by Lindsey. That fueled a fast break that Davis punctuated by dunking a lob from Teague to put the Cats ahead 42-27, prompting a St. John's timeout with 16:26 left.

The only unknown was the final score and whether Davis would achieve a triple-double. His teammates urged him to get the UK rarity. Only Chris Mills, another freshman, did it, scoring 19 points, grabbing 10 rebounds and handing out 10 assists against Austin Peay on Dec. 27, 1988.

Davis said he had "seven or eight" triple-doubles as a high school player.

"This is way different from high school," he said. "Players know how to adjust to it."■

St. John's player Sir'Dominic Pointer tried to shoot past Michael Kidd-Gilchrist and Anthony Davis in the first half in Lexington. *Pablo Alcalá | Lexington Herald-Leader*

BOX SCORE

ST. JOHN'S

## Player Name	TOT-FG FG-FGA	3-PT FG-FGA	FT-FTA	REBOUNDS OF	DE	TOT	PF	TP	A	TO	BLK	S	MIN
03 Achiuwa, God'sgift.. f	6-15	0-0	6-9	5	5	10	4	18	1	1	2	0	38
01 Greene, Phil........ g	3-9	0-2	2-2	0	3	3	1	8	3	0	0	0	29
04 Harkless, Moe....... g	4-12	0-2	8-10	2	8	10	4	16	0	5	3	3	35
10 Lindsey, Nurideen... g	0-3	0-0	1-3	0	0	0	5	1	1	5	0	0	20
11 Harrison, D'Angelo.. g	2-9	1-6	0-0	0	2	2	2	5	0	3	0	1	29
15 Pointer, Sir'Dominic	3-8	1-2	2-3	2	5	7	3	9	1	0	1	2	28
31 Stith, Malik........	1-4	0-1	0-0	2	1	3	1	2	3	1	0	0	21
TEAM...............				6	2	8				4			
Totals.............	19-60	2-13	19-27	17	26	43	20	59	9	19	6	6	200

TOTAL FG%	1st Half:	8-27 29.6%	2nd Half:	11-33 33.3%	Game:	31.7%	DEADB
3-Pt. FG%	1st Half:	0-7 0.0%	2nd Half:	2-6 33.3%	Game:	15.4%	REBS
F Throw %	1st Half:	4-6 66.7%	2nd Half:	15-21 71.4%	Game:	70.4%	4,1

KENTUCKY

## Player Name	TOT-FG FG-FGA	3-PT FG-FGA	FT-FTA	REBOUNDS OF	DE	TOT	PF	TP	A	TO	BLK	S	MIN
03 Jones, Terrence..... f	7-12	1-2	11-16	4	5	9	4	26	0	3	4	4	32
14 Kidd-Gilchrist, M... f	1-7	1-1	2-2	0	2	2	4	5	1	3	0	1	22
23 Davis, Anthony...... f	6-10	0-0	3-6	7	8	15	3	15	0	1	8	2	32
20 Lamb, Doron......... g	6-11	2-3	2-2	1	3	4	1	16	3	1	1	0	35
25 Teague, Marquis..... g	2-9	1-3	0-1	1	4	5	2	5	5	2	1	2	31
01 Miller, Darius......	4-10	0-5	1-1	2	2	4	2	9	6	1	1	0	27
13 Malone, Sam.........	0-1	0-0	0-0	0	0	0	0	0	1	1	0	0	2
30 Vargas, Eloy........	1-4	0-0	1-2	2	1	3	1	3	0	0	2	0	5
32 Long, Brian.........	0-0	0-0	0-0	0	0	0	0	0	0	0	0	0	2
33 Wiltjer, Kyle.......	1-5	0-2	0-0	0	3	3	1	2	0	0	1	0	12
TEAM...............				3		3							
Totals.............	28-69	5-16	20-30	20	28	48	18	81	16	12	18	9	200

TOTAL FG%	1st Half:	13-31 41.9%	2nd Half:	15-38 39.5%	Game:	40.6%	DEADB
3-Pt. FG%	1st Half:	2-9 22.2%	2nd Half:	3-7 42.9%	Game:	31.3%	REBS
F Throw %	1st Half:	3-7 42.9%	2nd Half:	17-23 73.9%	Game:	66.7%	4

Officials: Doug Shows, Les Jones, Jim Burr

Technical fouls: St. Johns University — Harrison, D'Angelo. Kentucky — None.

Attendance: 24,119

Score by Periods	1st	2nd	Total
St. John's University	20	39	59
Kentucky	31	50	81

Above: Anthony Davis dunked in the first half. *Pablo Alcalá | Lexington Herald-Leader*

Far Left: Doron Lamb was fouled by St. John's Nurideen Lindsey in the second half in Rupp Arena. *Pablo Alcalá | Lexington Herald-Leader*

Left: John Calipari reacted to a call against his team in the first half. *Pablo Alcalá | Lexington Herald-Leader*

#1 DARIUS MILLER

BY: MARK STORY | WILDCAT FEATURE

THE REASON TO STAY TRUE BLUE

UK's 4-year stalwart, Miller let Mason Co. ditch its Orange

There is always extra scrutiny on in-state basketball players who sign with Kentucky. Yet for Darius Miller, wearing the UK blue-and-white came with an extra load.

Miller's presence at Kentucky came at a time when his basketball-mad home, Mason County, had seen its feelings hurt by UK. In 2004, Kentucky declined to offer a scholarship to Mason County star Chris Lofton. The spurned guard went on to become a star at Tennessee.

In 2006, to reward the school that made a spot for one of their own, Maysville held a celebration of Lofton. Then-UT coach Bruce Pearl came to speak. The town decked itself out in UT orange. When Pearl entered the Mason County gymnasium, the high school pep band played Rocky Top.

In reaction, at least some Kentucky fans in the rest of the state were up in arms. Famously, one called a Lexington radio sports talk show to propose that the Ohio River be rerouted in such a way as to detach Mason County from the rest of the commonwealth.

"There are a lot of UK fans back home. There have been since I was little," Miller said. "Some of them, I guess, kind of changed over to Tennessee fans when Chris didn't get to come here."

When Miller got the chance that Lofton didn't — to sign with UK — he not only faced the pressure of an in-state player playing at Kentucky but carried the status of one-man peace delegation between his state university and his hoops-loving hometown.

Billy G.'s 'mind games'

Darius Miller is old-school. In a one-and-done world, Miller has had a throwback UK career. He has played four seasons, and gotten better every year.

When UK faces Georgia Thursday night in Rupp Arena, the 6-foot-8 Miller and fellow senior Eloy Vargas will run through the hoops and be serenaded with My Old Kentucky Home as part of Kentucky's traditional senior send-off.

"I don't know if I'll cry," Miller said. "Even if I want to,

Darius Miller reacted after hitting a shot as No. 1 Kentucky played No. 5 North Carolina in Lexington. *Mark Cornelison | Lexington Herald-Leader*

I don't know if I will let myself. But it is going to be an emotional time. I've been here a long time and been through a lot."

Miller played his freshman year (5.3 points, 3.1 rebounds) under Billy Gillispie. It was a turbulent time. Kentucky lost (22-14) far more often than Kentucky is accustomed to losing, and wound up in the NIT.

An adherent of Bob Knight-style motivational techniques, Gillispie frequently directed his cajoling toward Miller, a player perceived to have a high skill level but a sometimes passive approach.

"It's very difficult when someone is playing mind games with you every day," Brian Miller, Darius's father, said. "There's no question, that was a challenging year."

It ended with Gillispie being fired and John Calipari hired. Cal brought an immediate and dramatic enhancement in Kentucky's talent level.

As a sophomore, Miller (6.5 points, 2.5 rebounds) played a supporting role on a team led by freshman stars John Wall, DeMarcus Cousins and Eric Bledsoe.

After that season ended one victory short of the Final Four, UK sent five early entrants into the first round of the NBA Draft. So as a junior, Miller had to adapt to a new crop of lavishly hyped freshmen, Brandon Knight, Terrence Jones and Doron Lamb.

Interestingly, for two coaches as different as Gillispie and Calipari, both have faced the same challenge with Miller. Impelling the player to allow his talent to surmount what sometimes seems a self-imposed passivity.

When Miller threw down a monster slam this season in a victory over Mississippi, Calipari said "that dunk was one of the biggest plays I've ever seen him make. My point is, if you can do that, why isn't that you (all the time)?"

Becoming UK's 'Closer'

In a sense, the moment of truth in Miller's UK career came during his junior season at Mississippi.

With Kentucky clinging to a one-point lead late in the game but with the shot clock winding down, Miller twice had open looks for potential game-clinching shots - but passed both up. UK wound up with a rushed three-point shot from DeAndre Liggins that missed. Ole Miss won on a Chris Warren three-pointer.

It is a moment that could have broken Miller. Instead, it seemed to turn his UK career for the better.

Down the stretch of his junior season (10.9 points, 4.6 rebounds), Miller was a force. He scored in double figures in 10 straight games. He earned SEC Tournament MVP honors.

Facing North Carolina in the 2011 NCAA East Regional finals with the Final Four at stake, Miller was an unsung hero who made several big plays that helped Kentucky return to college basketball's biggest stage for the first time since 1998.

This season began with another Calipari talent infusion of freshmen, including Anthony Davis, Michael Kidd-Gilchrist and Marquis Teague.

A senior who had been a starter on a Final Four team, Miller was asked to come off the bench with Kidd-Gilchrist starting at small forward. He could have balked. Miller accepted the sixth-man role without complaint.

"I love Darius Miller for who he is," Kidd-Gilchrist said. "He's a brother to me now."

As a senior, Miller has emerged as something of Kentucky's Mariano Rivera: The guy who closes out victories.

In tight road wins at Vanderbilt and at Mississippi State and in a close home victory over Vandy, the Mason County product hit big shots down the stretch.

"He's staying confident no matter how many times he misses," UK forward Terrence Jones said of Miller. "I think that is the best change about his game, not worrying about his last shot, and he just keeps shooting."

Said Calipari: "I'm really proud of the strides (Miller's) made as far as being assertive."

Healing Mason's wounds

Miller is set to leave Kentucky with an impressive array of achievements. He is already a member of the 1,000-point club. He is the only Kentucky player to play in every game of what is currently a 51-contest home winning streak.

If, as many expect, UK wins the school's eighth NCAA championship in 2012, Miller will become the first player in state history to win a Kentucky boys' high school state championship, Mr. Basketball honors (he did both at Mason County in 2008) and an NCAA title at UK.

(Ex-Male High and Louisville star Darrell Griffith is the only male player ever to hit the "triple crown" of Kentucky basketball anywhere.)

Darius Miller scored two of his 12 points against North Carolina in Rupp Arena. *Mark Cornelison | Lexington Herald-Leader*

And, yes, in his hometown, Miller's success at UK does seem to have healed any lingering ill will toward the state university that followed Kentucky's snub of Chris Lofton.

Steve Appelman, the Mason County High School principal, says folks in Maysville have pulled out all the stops this winter trying to get tickets to see Miller play for Kentucky in Rupp Arena while they still can.

"I know people have been on StubHub, hitting up state legislators, anything they can think of," Appelman said. "I know people were hurt with what happened with Chris, but you might say time and Darius have healed those wounds."

Danny Weddle, longtime radio play-by-play voice of Mason County sports, said "some people here thought (Miller) should have gotten to start this year, but the way he handled that himself did a lot to lay that to rest. Mostly, people here just want number eight and are excited that Darius is such a big part of that."

Chris O'Hearn, the Mason County boys' hoops coach, said Miller "has done everything you are supposed to do in college. He stayed four years. He's going to get his degree. He's gotten better every year. Whether he's started or not starting, he's been totally unselfish and totally a team-first guy."

Now, thanks to Darius Miller, there are no more calls on Lexington talk radio for a massive water project to reroute the Ohio River and cut off Mason County from Kentucky.

"Hopefully, after Chris, fans back home switched back over (to UK) with me," Miller said. "Me being here, it means a lot to them. It meant a lot to me, too, knowing how important it is to them."■

VS. NORTH CAROLINA

WILDCATS	73
TAR HEELS	72

RUPP ARENA DECEMBER 3, 2011

BY: JOHN CLAY REGULAR SEASON

UK STOPS UNC IN BATTLE THAT MATCHES THE HYPE

Let's make it best-of-seven.

Let's play it right here, right now, this season, these players, these coaches, these Kentucky Wildcats, these North Carolina Tar Heels, these fans, a best-of-seven to decide the basketball champion of the world.

That's what it felt like Saturday at high noon in Rupp Arena, where it might have been student-athletes on the floor with NCAA logos on their jerseys, but the feel was all big-time professional, with future millionaires playing for pride and honor and the joy of coming out on top.

Turned out, we were the ones who came out on top because we're the ones who got lucky with Saturday's dramatic 73-72 Kentucky win over North Carolina before an overflow crowd of 24,398.

Not much in our society matches the hype anymore. We're resigned to the big letdown. Over-sold and over-blown. Not this time. The Rumble in Rupp was 120 glorious minutes of everything we hoped it would be.

"We were excited to play them, they were excited to play us," said UK senior Darius Miller. "It turned out to be the game that everybody wanted."

There's nothing like March Madness, no doubt, with its Cinderella stories, but when it comes to twin towers of power, maybe David Stern and his NBA brethren have it right. With two teams as good and as talented as this, don't you want to see them bang heads again and again and again?

"There were some very talented and gifted youngsters out there," said the losing coach, Roy Williams.

Thing was, the glamour guys played like gritty guys. This was no posing, just performing. These

Above: Marquis Teague celebrated the final seconds of Kentucky's win over North Carolina in an early-season battle of college basketball titans. *Mark Cornelison | Lexington Herald-Leader*

Right: Anthony Davis soared into the picture to block the last-second shot attempt of North Carolina's John Henson. No. 1 Kentucky held on for the 73-72 win in Lexington. *Mark Cornelison | Lexington Herald-Leader*

DAVIS
23
UK
NORTH
11
CAROLINA
BARNES
40

were all 10 players on the floor playing as hard as they could before a crowd screaming as loud as they could.

They probably could have heard the screams all the way to Chapel Hill when UK's Anthony Davis elevated and blocked John Henson's baseline jumper on the game's final play.

North Carolina won the first half by five points. Kentucky won the second half by six. North Carolina made six of nine three-pointers in the first 20 minutes. Kentucky shot 56 percent from the floor in the second 20 minutes. The final outcome was decided by a single point. Both teams gave as good as they got.

OK, OK, as proven by Ohio State's demolition of Duke last week, the Buckeyes are really good. And you can give Duke a mulligan, what with the Blue Devils globe-trotting from Madison Square Garden to Maui and then Columbus.

Meanwhile, if Syracuse can somehow avoid the distractions and keep their coach, the Orange have to be counted among the nation's four or five best outfits.

And, yeah, we know, North Carolina had already coughed up their No. 1 ranking by losing last week to UNLV, turning the top spot over to John Calipari's Cats.

"We didn't play nearly this well last Saturday night," said UNC Coach Roy Williams.

Still, it would be difficult to come away from Saturday not thinking what we thought before the season, that these are the two best teams in the country.

Guard Doron Lamb scored two of his 14 points against North Carolina.
Mark Cornelison | Lexington Herald-Leader

With three freshmen playing such pivotal roles, Kentucky figures to get nothing but better.

Even though North Carolina is older, there's every reason to believe the Tar Heels will climb the improvement ladder. Every team is different just as every year is different, after all, and even veteran teams have to find their own way.

Now, we just need these two to find each other again later this season.

If we can't do it six more times, hopefully we can do it one more.

"We know they're going to be there," said Miller when asked about March. "They're a very talented team, a very experienced team. They're probably going to be there at the end."

"Let's hope if we have to play them again," Calipari said, "it's the very last game of the season, for both teams, in one place, and that's when we play them again."■

Above: Anthony Davis pulled down the ball after his last-second shot block against North Carolina. *Mark Cornelison | Lexington Herald-Leader*

Below: Terrence Jones reacted to a Kentucky run against North Carolina in Rupp Arena. *Mark Cornelison | Lexington Herald-Leader*

BOX SCORE

NORTH CAROLINA

## Player Name	TOT-FG FG-FGA	3-PT FG-FGA	FT-FTA	REBOUNDS OF	DE	TOT	PF	TP	A	TO	BLK	S	MIN
31 Henson, John........ f	4-11	0-0	2-2	3	5	8	1	10	1	2	3	0	33
40 Barnes, Harrison.... f	5-12	4-5	0-0	1	1	2	3	14	0	1	1	0	24
44 Zeller, Tyler....... f	4-9	0-0	6-6	5	3	8	1	14	2	4	1	1	28
01 Strickland, Dexter.. g	2-6	0-0	1-2	1	2	3	1	5	5	2	0	0	28
05 Marshall, Kendall... g	3-6	2-4	0-0	1	1	2	3	8	8	3	1	1	35
15 Hairston, P.J.......	3-4	3-4	2-2	0	0	0	1	11	0	1	0	0	14
24 Watts, Justin.......	0-1	0-0	0-0	0	1	1	2	0	0	0	0	0	4
35 Bullock, Reggie.....	3-8	2-5	0-0	2	3	5	1	8	1	0	0	0	19
43 McAdoo, James M.....	1-3	0-0	0-2	0	4	4	3	2	0	0	0	0	15
TEAM...............				2	1	3							
Totals.............	25-60	11-18	11-14	15	21	36	16	72	17	13	6	2	200

TOTAL FG%	1st Half:	15-31 48.4%	2nd Half:	10-29 34.5%	Game:	41.7%	DEADB
3-Pt. FG%	1st Half:	6-9 66.7%	2nd Half:	5-9 55.6%	Game:	61.1%	REBS
F Throw %	1st Half:	7-8 87.5%	2nd Half:	4-6 66.7%	Game:	78.6%	1

KENTUCKY

## Player Name	TOT-FG FG-FGA	3-PT FG-FGA	FT-FTA	REBOUNDS OF	DE	TOT	PF	TP	A	TO	BLK	S	MIN
03 Jones, Terrence..... f	5-14	1-5	3-3	4	3	7	2	14	1	1	3	2	35
14 Kidd-Gilchrist, M... f	6-10	0-1	5-7	4	7	11	2	17	1	1	1	1	33
23 Davis, Anthony...... f	3-6	0-2	1-1	2	7	9	2	7	1	1	2	2	34
20 Lamb, Doron......... g	6-12	2-3	0-0	2	2	4	2	14	2	4	0	1	34
25 Teague, Marquis..... g	3-11	0-4	1-3	0	2	2	2	7	4	1	0	0	30
01 Miller, Darius......	4-8	1-2	3-4	1	0	1	2	12	0	1	0	1	23
30 Vargas, Eloy........	0-1	0-0	0-0	1	1	2	0	0	0	0	1	0	6
33 Wiltjer, Kyle.......	1-1	0-0	0-0	0	0	0	0	2	0	0	0	0	5
TEAM...............				2		2							
Totals.............	28-63	4-17	13-18	16	22	38	12	73	9	9	7	7	200

TOTAL FG%	1st Half:	14-38 36.8%	2nd Half:	14-25 56.0%	Game:	44.4%	DEADB
3-Pt. FG%	1st Half:	2-9 22.2%	2nd Half:	2-8 25.0%	Game:	23.5%	REBS
F Throw %	1st Half:	8-12 66.7%	2nd Half:	5-6 83.3%	Game:	72.2%	3

Officials: Tony Greene, Mike Nance, Ron Groover

Technical fouls: North Carolina — None. Kentucky — None.

Attendance: 24,398

Score by Periods	1st	2nd	Total
North Carolina	43	29	72
Kentucky	38	35	73

Above: John Calipari talked with forward Michael Kidd-Gilchrist as No. 1 Kentucky played No. 5 North Carolina in Lexington. *Mark Cornelison | Lexington Herald-Leader*

AT INDIANA

HOOSIERS 73
WILDCATS 72

ASSEMBLY HALL DECEMBER 10, 2011

BY: JERRY TIPTON REGULAR SEASON

RED ALERT: INDIANA'S BACK

Hoosiers knock off No. 1 Kentucky on Watford's buzzer-beating three

Because he hadn't been here in five years, the Pied Piper of college basketball, Dick Vitale, had to ask before the game where ESPN's telecast team would sit. That half decade represented the time Indiana had wandered the roundball wilderness.

Assembly Hall, which IU calls the Carnegie Hall of the sport, rocked like a cellar full of noise Saturday. In this big red canyon of an arena, the Hoosiers sought to end their irrelevancy by beating No. 1 Kentucky.

Junior forward Christian Watford became IU's Moses by hitting a three-pointer at the buzzer to beat Kentucky 73-72 Saturday.

The shot from the left wing sent a red sea of delirious Hoosier fans stampeding to the court and a stunned Kentucky team slowly retreating to the locker room.

IU Coach Tom Crean said he took time to absorb what he called "one of those moments everybody's going to remember."

UK Coach John Calipari said he was proud of his inexperienced team giving itself a chance to win despite the most electric homecourt disadvantage Kentucky has faced in years.

"I'm speechless," IU's Victor Oladipo said in the safety of the post-game interview room. "Did you see how many people were in there? I couldn't see my mother. It was so loud, my head is still hurting."

For Kentucky, which rallied from a nine-point deficit with less than eight minutes left, the defeat was partially self-inflicted.

Doron Lamb (20) walked to the bench after missing a free throw at the end of the game. *Mark Cornelison | Lexington Herald-Leader*

Terrence Jones got stripped on his way up by Indiana forward Cody Zeller (40) as No. 1 Kentucky played Indiana in Bloomington. *Mark Cornelison | Lexington Herald-Leader*

Marquis Teague's drive by Jordan Hulls — UK attacked IU's guards all day — gave Kentucky a 71-70 lead with 48.8 seconds left.

The Cats missed a chance to extend that lead when Anthony Davis missed his only free throw attempt, the front end of a one-and-one with 19 seconds left.

Indiana called time with 13.9 seconds left to plot the winner. But Oladipo lost the ball on the drive, giving UK another chance to seal it.

This time Doron Lamb missed the first of two free throws with 5.6 seconds left. IU called time.

After Lamb made the second, IU rushed upcourt, handing the ball to Watford on the left wing. He rose immediately and swished the shot.

"We were going to foul," Calipari said. "We had two fouls to use. So the whole time out was about fouling."

But UK, which was whistled for four second-half fouls, did not foul.

"When Marquis tried to foul and they didn't call it, no one fouled," Calipari said. "... I have no idea what went through our minds. Maybe they thought, 'I'm not fouling. Time will run out.' I don't know."

Indiana (9-0) expected Kentucky to foul.

"That was the first thing (assistant) Coach (Tim) Buckley told me," said Verdell Jones, who made the pass to Watford. "He just missed me."

Watford, who inbounded the ball, led all scorers with 20 points. "When I took the ball out, I guess they kind of forgot abut me," he said.

Inbounding the ball from under UK's offensive basket made precise planning impossible. "We couldn't draw any big play," freshman standout Cody Zeller said.

When UK prevented a long inbounds, IU improvised. Watford's shot arched high in the air, counter-clockwise rotation tight, and zipped through as the buzzer sounded.

"The vivid image for me was how picture perfect the shot was," Crean said. "... A perfectly fundamentally formed shot."

As against North Carolina last weekend, Kentucky trailed at halftime. But the 30-29 margin represented a triumph of sorts given UK's foul trouble, a missing-in-action Terrence Jones and the eight-point deficit with less than two minutes left in the half.

A sign of an unusual and inspired opponent came early when Zeller blocked Michael Kidd-Gilchrist's usually automatic drive in transition.

An 11-0 run put Indiana ahead 45-35 with 15:55 left. Will Sheehey capped the run with a rhythm three-pointer in transition.

Terrence Jones put up a shot in traffic against Indiana.
Mark Cornelison | Lexington Herald-Leader

Although Jones' funk and Davis' foul trouble continued, Kentucky did not roll over.

Trailing 66-57 with less than eight minutes left, Kentucky turned up the defense. IU missed seven straight shots, going scoreless for more than four minutes.

Kentucky slowly chipped into the deficit, closing within 66-65 on Kidd-Gilchrist's post-up with 4:09 left.

After a timeout, Indiana went to Watford, who drove by Jones for a layup. That continued Jones' miserable afternoon and set up the dramatic finish.

Of the game-winner, Verdell Jones noted how Watford served as a trailer. Crean believed his senior guard would drive for a shot.

But Verdell Jones heard Watford.

"He yelled 'V! V!,'" Verdell Jones said. "I passed to him. The rest was history."■

BOX SCORE

KENTUCKY

## Player Name	TOT-FG FG-FGA	3-PT FG-FGA	FT-FTA	REBOUNDS OF	DE	TOT	PF	TP	A	TO	BLK	S	MIN
03 Jones, Terrence..... f	2-3	0-0	0-2	0	1	1	0	4	1	6	2	1	28
14 Kidd-Gilchrist, M... f	9-12	0-0	0-0	4	5	9	1	18	0	2	1	2	38
23 Davis, Anthony...... f	3-4	0-0	0-1	2	7	9	4	6	1	1	3	3	24
20 Lamb, Doron......... g	5-14	2-3	7-11	1	0	1	2	19	1	1	1	2	36
25 Teague, Marquis..... g	6-11	0-1	3-3	0	1	1	2	15	5	3	0	1	31
01 Miller, Darius......	4-8	0-3	0-0	0	2	2	3	8	0	2	0	0	26
30 Vargas, Eloy........	1-2	0-0	0-0	2	1	3	0	2	0	0	0	1	10
33 Wiltjer, Kyle.......	0-0	0-0	0-0	0	0	0	1	0	1	1	0	0	7
TEAM................				1	3	4				1			
Totals.............	30-54	2-7	10-17	10	20	30	13	72	9	17	7	10	200

TOTAL FG%	1st Half: 13-29 44.8%	2nd Half: 17-25 68.0%	Game: 55.6%	DEADB
3-Pt. FG%	1st Half: 2-6 33.3%	2nd Half: 0-1 0.0%	Game: 28.6%	REBS
F Throw %	1st Half: 1-4 25.0%	2nd Half: 9-13 69.2%	Game: 58.8%	5

INDIANA

## Player Name	TOT-FG FG-FGA	3-PT FG-FGA	FT-FTA	REBOUNDS OF	DE	TOT	PF	TP	A	TO	BLK	S	MIN
02 Watford, Christian.. f	8-15	4-6	0-0	1	4	5	2	20	1	1	0	1	30
40 Zeller, Cody........ f	4-8	0-0	3-3	5	2	7	2	11	1	3	1	1	37
01 Hulls, Jordan....... g	4-7	3-6	0-0	0	2	2	3	11	5	5	0	4	35
04 Oladipo, Victor..... g	4-12	0-0	5-6	3	4	7	2	13	1	3	1	0	32
12 Jones III, Verdell.. g	2-7	0-1	4-5	2	2	4	2	8	3	5	0	1	34
10 Sheehey, Will.......	3-8	2-2	2-2	1	0	1	3	10	0	0	0	0	16
11 Moore, Daniel.......	0-0	0-0	0-1	0	0	0	1	0	0	0	0	0	5
25 Pritchard, Tom......	0-1	0-0	0-0	0	2	2	1	0	1	1	0	0	11
TEAM................				2		2							
Totals.............	25-58	9-15	14-17	14	16	30	16	73	12	18	2	7	200

TOTAL FG%	1st Half: 9-24 37.5%	2nd Half: 16-34 47.1%	Game: 43.1%	DEADB
3-Pt. FG%	1st Half: 2-6 33.3%	2nd Half: 7-9 77.8%	Game: 60.0%	REBS
F Throw %	1st Half: 10-12 83.3%	2nd Half: 4-5 80.0%	Game: 82.4%	2

Officials: Ted Valentine, Mike Kitts, Tom Eades

Technical fouls: Kentucky — None. Indiana — None.

Attendance: 17,472

Score by Periods	1st	2nd	Total
Kentucky	29	43	72
Indiana	30	43	73

Above: Indiana guard Victor Oladipo hugged Christian Watford (2) after he hit the game-winning shot as Indiana beat No. 1 Kentucky 73-72 in Bloomington. *Mark Cornelison | Lexington Herald-Leader*

Left: Darius Miller left the floor as Indiana fans stormed the court. *Mark Cornelison | Lexington Herald-Leader*

#3 TERRENCE JONES

BY: JERRY TIPTON

WILDCAT FEATURE

JONES RESTORES ORDER FOR CATS

Sophomore rediscovers freshman form

Marquis Teague missed a driving shot late in Kentucky's 74-50 victory at Louisiana State on Saturday. As if on a pogo stick, Terrence Jones went up for the rebound once, twice, thrice. Finally, Jones tipped in a fourth attempt.

UK Coach John Calipari suggested it was a significant moment brilliantly disguised in the mind-numbing final minutes of a blowout.

"When a guy is going for the ball four straight jumps, c'mon," Calipari said. "That's what we've all been waiting for."

Jones, the Southeastern Conference's Pre-season Player of the Year and its mid-season enigma, at long last looked like his old self. Or, better put, his young self as Kentucky's freshman star last season.

Jones scored a season-high 27 points and grabbed nine rebounds, barely missing his first double-double of the season. He blocked three shots and made two steals. A 7-for-16 free-throw shooter the previous two games, he hit seven of eight foul shots against LSU.

Numbers aside, Jones transformed Kentucky from superior, as it's No. 1 ranking suggests, to perhaps that exceptional level reserved for Kentucky's national championship teams.

"He makes us different," said Calipari, saying a lot without saying a lot.

When asked about the play in which Jones repeatedly leaped, Calipari said, "That's the guy I want. That's the guy people want to see. That's the kind of guy people want to play with and coach. ...

"That wins. That other guy, you lose with."

That other guy was the Jones who seemed to struggle all season to find his bearings. Of course, the nadir came at Indiana, where Calipari benched Jones in the final minutes of a game that required both teams to search their souls for hidden reserves of resolve.

"Some guys, they stepped up and took on the challenge more than older guys," Jones said of Kentucky's freshman stars this season.

Terrence Jones was all smiles as he led all scorers with 20 points in a win over South Carolina. *Mark Cornelison | Lexington Herald-Leader*

At LSU, Jones answered Calipari's repeated appeals to put his stamp on this Kentucky team.

"He just takes a lot of pressure off all these young kids, and he needs to," Calipari said.

Repeating a theme he's mentioned in his two earlier seasons as UK coach, Calipari said veterans must lead the way as the grind of a season enters the time to make memories or fade away.

"Freshmen, you can't expect them to carry the load," Calipari said. "At times, we've been doing that."

Terrence Jones celebrated a three-pointer that forced an LSU time out during their game in Baton Rouge, La. *Mark Cornelison | Lexington Herald-Leader*

Kentucky, which improved to 21-1 overall and an SEC-best 7-0, broke it open about midway through the game. In a nine-minute segment that included 13 straight points by Jones, the Cats exploded a 25-24 first-half lead to a 52-30 suffocation with 14 minutes to play.

Freshman point guard Teague saw a hot hand to feed and kept feeding it.

"He was scoring at will pretty much in the post," Teague said of Jones.

LSU (12-9, 2-5 SEC), followed the course of many Kentucky opponents. The Tigers tried to push UK around. If there had been a three-knockdown rule, star freshman Anthony Davis would have been a technical knockout.

Enter Jones, who said he drew strength from Malcolm White's flagrant-foul take-down of Davis.

"The only way we can redeem that is by continuing to play hard," Jones said.

Calipari suggested that no UK player was better equipped to be the redeemer than Jones, a 6-foot-9, 252-pound dynamo this day.

" 'Terrence, you negate it better than anybody we play,' " Calipari said he told Jones. " 'Now, go play. Want the contact. You create the contact. You go be physical in there.'

"He can do it. He just has to want to do it."

In the first half, Kentucky showed it could vary from its customary inside scoring.

Even though three of LSU's players picked up two fouls each inside the first nine minutes, Kentucky somehow managed to get outscored 8-6 in the paint. Freshman Johnny O'Bryant III accounted for six of LSU's points and none of the fouls. He finished with 12 points and nine rebounds.

LSU closed within one, 25-24, when freshman Anthony Hickey's fast-break lob led to a dunk by Storm Warren. That was one of the few highlights for Hickey, Kentucky's Mr. Basketball last season, who didn't score until the 9:47 mark of the second half.

Kentucky re-established inside dominance after intermission. Barely two minutes into the second half, the Cats — or rather, Jones — matched the six points from the paint of the first half.

UK exceeded that production when Jones posted up for a basket with 17:02 left.

Miller described the impact of an active, engaged Jones as "a huge difference."

"He's like the key part of the team, one of the best players," he said. "When he gets it going, it makes it a lot easier for everybody else. It opens up stuff for everybody else when they've got to double-team him."

Calipari called the Jones-led performance the best Kentucky has played. "We beat anybody playing this way," he said.

LSU Coach Trent Johnson suggested it might have been the first of several opportunities for Louisianians to see a stellar Kentucky team in the flesh.

"They will be back in New Orleans, probably twice," he said, a reference to the upcoming SEC Tournament and Final Four. "... Let's not over-analyze this. Let's not just critique my kids. Because sometimes you have to tip your hat to who is better."■

WILDCATS 69
CARDINALS 62

RUPP ARENA — DECEMBER 31, 2011

BY: JOHN CLAY — REGULAR SEASON

KIDD-GILCHRIST PROVES METTLE ON BIG STAGE

In a man's game Saturday afternoon at Rupp Arena, Michael Kidd-Gilchrist wasn't just the man. He was Superman.

He was the one leaping over tall defenders in a single bound for a rebound, flying faster than a speeding bullet up the floor on a fast break, more powerful than a locomotive on a baseline drive through a thicket of defenders.

In a game of a combined 52 fouls, 70 free throws and 35 turnovers, the Kentucky freshman was the shining star of the long, hard slog.

He scored 24 points and grabbed 19 rebounds as Kentucky beat Louisville for the third consecutive season, this time 69-62.

"He wasn't bothered as much as some of the others by the physical play," said John Calipari, his record now 3-0 as the current Kentucky coach against the former Kentucky coach. "He almost relished it and just want after it. That's why he played the way he did."

Said Kidd-Gilchrist, "I was built for this."

Kentucky and Louisville might represent the upper stratosphere of college basketball rivalries, a pair of storied programs in the nation's most basketball-crazed state.

There was the rap star Jay-Z, taking a break from the pregnant Beyoncé, to sit across from the UK bench. There was Ashley Judd in her trademark Kentucky T-shirt waving to the crowd. There was Clark Kellogg and the national CBS cameras.

But Saturday's showdown wasn't contested so much in the celestial stars as down on basketball's mean streets, with plenty of elbows and forearms and shrieking whistles.

Michael Kidd-Gilchrist celebrated UK's win over Louisville. *Mark Cornelison | Lexington Herald-Leader*

Louisville was called for 29 fouls. Kentucky was called for 23. Louisville's Chane Behanan, the Bowling Green freshman who previously had boasted that the Cardinals were the nation's best team, picked up a first-half technical foul and ultimately fouled out.

Not to be left out, Calipari earned a second-half technical which had the hyperventilating UK coach nearly out to mid-court to protest a perceived wrong.

Terrence Jones scored against Louisville. *Jonathan Palmer | Lexington Herald-Leader*

Did you expect this to be a game with so many fouls called?

"Oh, yeah," said Calipari. "I would hope they would be called."

Its roster comparatively short of talent, Louisville no doubt wanted a slower, physical game. But because of that strategy, the intensity of the rivalry and perhaps the officials' desire to keep emotions from escalating into a Xavier- Cincinnati Crosstown Punch-out, the game had little to no rhythm.

There were 119 shots taken in the game. Just 37 were made. Louisville shot 32.3 percent, including 25.7 percent the second half.

Kentucky ended up shooting 29.8 percent.

And won.

It was the first time since Dec. 6, 2003, against UCLA in Anaheim, Calif., that a UK basketball team had made less than 30 percent of its shots and walked off the floor a winner.

How?

"You defend and rebound, and you win anyway," Calipari said. "And that's what we want to do."

That's what Kidd-Gilchrist wants to do. The 6-foot-7 New Jersey native compared himself to Tim Tebow the other day when asked about why he started the "Breakfast Club," in which teammates work out and have breakfast together before practice.

And though Jay-Z might have been in the house — he had Kidd-Gilchrist's jersey in his hand — MKG's all-out play makes you think of the DJ Khaled song Rupp played during pre-game, "All I do is win, win, win no matter what."

"And my mom was here," said Kidd-Gilchrist afterward.

It was just a little more than week ago that his mother, Cynthia, was in the hospital with a health scare. She is fine now, said her son, in fact healthy enough to travel to Lexington to be courtside.

"She smiled at me," said her son, admitting he had taken a peek at her during the game, "I had to smile back."

On a day in which he rose above all the others, Michael Kidd-Gilchrist wasn't alone.

Kentucky fans were smiling, too.■

Anthony Davis blocked the shot of Louisville guard Chris Smith, one of his 6 blocks in the game.
Mark Cornelison | Lexington Herald-Leader

BOX SCORE

LOUISVILLE

## Player Name	TOT-FG FG-FGA	3-PT FG-FGA	FT-FTA	REBOUNDS OF	DE	TOT	PF	TP	A	TO	BLK	S	MIN
14 Kuric, Kyle......... f	1-4	0-2	0-0	0	2	2	4	2	1	1	0	1	38
24 Behanan, Chane...... f	1-3	0-0	2-2	2	3	5	5	4	1	1	0	0	15
10 Dieng, Gorgui....... c	2-5	0-0	1-2	0	5	5	4	5	0	3	6	1	33
03 Siva, Peyton........ g	2-13	0-4	4-6	0	2	2	4	8	4	3	1	1	29
05 Smith, Chris........ g	2-10	1-3	2-2	2	1	3	3	7	0	0	0	3	21
02 Smith, Russ.........	10-20	3-8	7-10	2	3	5	3	30	0	3	0	3	27
04 Buckles, Rakeem.....	1-4	0-0	0-0	2	1	3	4	2	0	2	0	0	15
21 Swopshire, Jared....	1-2	0-1	2-3	0	2	2	2	4	0	0	1	3	17
22 Justice, Elisha.....	0-0	0-0	0-0	0	1	1	0	0	0	0	0	0	1
23 Ware, Kevin.........	0-1	0-0	0-2	0	0	0	0	0	0	1	0	0	4
TEAM................				2	1	3							
Totals..............	20-62	4-18	18-27	10	21	31	29	62	6	14	8	12	200

TOTAL FG%	1st Half:	11-27 40.7%	2nd Half:	9-35 25.7%	Game:	32.3%	DEADB
3-Pt. FG%	1st Half:	1-5 20.0%	2nd Half:	3-13 23.1%	Game:	22.2%	REBS
F Throw %	1st Half:	10-14 71.4%	2nd Half:	8-13 61.5%	Game:	66.7%	3,4

KENTUCKY

## Player Name	TOT-FG FG-FGA	3-PT FG-FGA	FT-FTA	REBOUNDS OF	DE	TOT	PF	TP	A	TO	BLK	S	MIN
14 Kidd-Gilchrist, M... f	7-16	2-4	8-13	6	13	19	3	24	1	0	0	0	39
23 Davis, Anthony...... f	3-4	0-0	12-13	2	8	10	3	18	0	2	6	3	27
01 Miller, Darius...... g	2-8	1-3	2-2	3	1	4	4	7	1	8	0	0	32
20 Lamb, Doron......... g	1-7	0-3	8-9	0	0	0	4	10	2	4	0	0	24
25 Teague, Marquis..... g	1-8	0-3	2-2	0	3	3	5	4	5	4	1	0	29
03 Jones, Terrence.....	1-9	0-1	0-4	3	8	11	1	2	0	1	0	3	30
10 Beckham, Twany......	0-0	0-0	0-0	0	0	0	0	0	1	0	0	0	2
30 Vargas, Eloy........	0-0	0-0	0-0	0	0	0	0	0	0	0	0	0	2
33 Wiltjer, Kyle.......	2-5	0-2	0-0	0	2	2	2	4	0	1	0	0	15
TEAM................				6	2	8	1			1			
Totals..............	17-57	3-16	32-43	20	37	57	23	69	10	21	7	6	200

TOTAL FG%	1st Half:	8-29 27.6%	2nd Half:	9-28 32.1%	Game:	29.8%	DEADB
3-Pt. FG%	1st Half:	3-9 33.3%	2nd Half:	0-7 0.0%	Game:	18.8%	REBS
F Throw %	1st Half:	17-23 73.9%	2nd Half:	15-20 75.0%	Game:	74.4%	6,1

Officials: Tony Greene, Jamie Luckie, Michael Stephens

Technical fouls: Louisville — Behanan, Chane. Kentucky — TEAM.

Attendance: 24,387

Score by Periods	1st	2nd	Total
Louisville	33	29	62
Kentucky	36	33	69

Above: Louisville's Russ Smith fouled Michael Kidd-Gilchrist as he drove toward the basket in the first half. *Pablo Alcalá | Lexington Herald-Leader*

Left: Kentucky's John Calipari greeted Louisville coach Rick Pitino before No. 3 Kentucky faced No. 4 Louisville in Lexington. *Mark Cornelison | Lexington Herald-Leader*

AT TENNESSEE

WILDCATS	65
VOLUNTEERS	62

THOMPSON-BOLING ARENA — JANUARY 14, 2012

BY: JOHN CLAY — REGULAR SEASON

CATS' SOLID SIX NOT 'SCARY' YET

Cal seeking Alabama-like precision

Imagine if they ever hit on all cylinders. Imagine if they did it all at the same time.

Imagine if they did it for all 40 minutes.

Imagine a basketball game in which Anthony Davis produces a triple-double, Darius Miller chases down every 50-50 ball, Terrence Jones flows effortlessly to the bucket, Doron Lamb drills every perimeter shot, Marquis Teague makes nothing but wise decisions, and where Michael Kidd-Gilchrist plays with so much fire he might spontaneously combust.

"It'd be scary," said John Calipari on Saturday after his young team rallied from a six-point halftime deficit to beat host Tennessee 65-62.

It would be Alabama football the night of the BCS championship game, a Nick Saban machine that made all the right plays at all the right times without a single mistake, or maybe one late in the game, after the outcome was decided, but one in which the coach still gets mad because he demands perfection.

"I hit it at one of the timeouts again; I talked about Alabama football again," Calipari said. "I said look, 'They executed. They executed. The other team was going wild, talking junk, hitting, shouldering, and Alabama focused on my job. They didn't worry about the talking and all the other stuff and the hoopla.' "

That's been the Kentucky coach's fabulous new obsession since he watched Bama bash LSU Monday night.

For any coach, it was the dream game: Execution. Physical play. No mistakes. A powerful machine. Roll Tide.

Calipari has the pieces. He knows it. We know it.

Above: Anthony Davis dunked in the first half of Kentucky's 65-62 win over Tennessee. *David Perry | Lexington Herald-Leader*

Right: Marquis Teague put up a shot over Tennessee's Kenny Hall in Knoxville. *David Perry | Lexington Herald-Leader*

BUY A TOYOTA
HALL
20
KENTUCKY
23
58
UT

Michael Kidd-Gilchrist drove to the basket against Tennessee. *David Perry | Lexington Herald-Leader*

But the pieces aren't all working together at the same time in the same game for the same long stretches. He knows that, too.

Before a capacity crowd of 21,678 at Thompson-Boling — many dressed in blue — Davis scored a game-high 18 points, including two with 57 seconds left on a face-the-basket jumper off a post move that even the freshman admitted he had never made before.

Kidd-Gilchrist returned to being a monster-in-motion, scoring 17 points, grabbing 12 rebounds, making the glorious hustle plays on both ends of the floor that helped Kentucky turn off Tennessee's faucet and hold the home team scoreless from the 6:56 mark till the Vols finally banged home a three with 37 ticks left.

"I've got a lot of heart," said Kidd-Gilchrist afterward.

Yes, Michael, we know. Boy, do we know.

The others have a lot of talent, and no doubt heart, but they don't yet possess whatever it takes to produce that consistency game after game.

"It starts with physical play," Calipari said. "If those guys will be more physical, they'll be more aggressive offensively, they'll make better plays. Simple. Everything happens from physical play."

Jones showed more signs of a consistent recovery from his December recession. The sophomore scored 10 points, grabbed five rebounds and blocked three shots before fouling out.

Calipari was complimentary of point guard Teague's defense and floor game, despite the

freshman's five turnovers.

Then you look at Lamb's stat line. The sophomore made just one of seven shots, scored just four points and missed the front end of a one-and-one from the foul line with 36.1 seconds left and the Cats gripping a five-point lead.

"Not a good day for him," said Calipari.

Miller scored four points and had just one rebound in 23 minutes. He didn't commit a turnover, but he didn't have an assist, either. His last three games, Miller has 17 points and six rebounds.

"We need the other guys to step up and ball," Calipari said. "For us to win on the road with Darius and Doron going 2-for-11, and literally throwing balls at the rim thinking they were going to get hit, 2-for-11, and Terrence showed signs, but they still roughed him up, and to still win. Think about that."

Better to dream about this: The night all six play to their potential.

That would be Crimson Tide scary.■

BOX SCORE

KENTUCKY

## Player Name	TOT-FG FG-FGA	3-PT FG-FGA	FT-FTA	REBOUNDS OF	DE	TOT	PF	TP	A	TO	BLK	S	MIN
03 Jones, Terrence..... f	4-8	0-1	2-3	2	3	5	5	10	1	3	3	1	24
14 Kidd-Gilchrist, M... f	4-11	1-1	8-12	6	6	12	1	17	1	2	1	3	39
23 Davis, Anthony...... f	7-10	0-0	4-5	2	6	8	2	18	2	0	4	2	35
01 Miller, Darius...... g	1-4	0-1	2-2	0	1	1	3	4	0	0	0	1	23
25 Teague, Marquis..... g	3-8	0-0	1-2	0	1	1	3	7	1	5	0	1	38
10 Beckham, Twany......	0-0	0-0	0-0	0	0	0	0	0	0	0	0	0	1
20 Lamb, Doron.........	1-7	0-1	2-3	0	4	4	2	4	2	2	0	0	28
30 Vargas, Eloy........	0-0	0-0	0-0	0	1	1	0	0	0	0	0	0	3
33 Wiltjer, Kyle.......	1-1	1-1	2-2	0	1	1	3	5	0	1	0	0	9
TEAM...............					2	2	1						
Totals.............	21-49	2-5	21-29	10	25	35	20	65	7	13	8	8	200

TOTAL FG%	1st Half:	9-25 36.0%	2nd Half:	12-24 50.0%	Game:	42.9%	DEADB
3-Pt. FG%	1st Half:	0-2 0.0%	2nd Half:	2-3 66.7%	Game:	40.0%	REBS
F Throw %	1st Half:	10-15 66.7%	2nd Half:	11-14 78.6%	Game:	72.4%	3

TENNESSEE

## Player Name	TOT-FG FG-FGA	3-PT FG-FGA	FT-FTA	REBOUNDS OF	DE	TOT	PF	TP	A	TO	BLK	S	MIN
03 Woolridge, Renaldo.. f	0-6	0-3	0-0	2	2	4	1	0	1	1	1	0	16
34 Maymon, Jeronne..... f	4-7	0-0	7-10	2	8	10	4	15	0	3	0	2	30
01 Richardson, Josh.... g	2-2	1-1	0-0	0	1	1	4	5	0	0	3	0	16
11 Golden, Trae........ g	1-6	0-3	0-0	0	1	1	2	2	6	2	0	0	31
23 Tatum, Cameron...... g	5-11	3-6	3-4	0	2	2	3	16	3	2	0	1	34
00 Makanjuola, Yemi....	0-0	0-0	0-0	0	1	1	1	0	0	0	0	0	2
05 Stokes, Jarnell.....	4-5	0-0	1-2	1	3	4	2	9	1	3	0	0	17
13 McBee, Skylar.......	2-4	2-4	0-0	0	3	3	1	6	0	1	0	1	25
20 Hall, Kenny.........	3-9	0-0	2-2	1	2	3	3	8	0	2	1	0	18
52 McRae, Jordan.......	0-2	0-0	1-2	0	0	0	1	1	1	1	0	0	11
TEAM...............				3		3							
Totals.............	21-52	6-17	14-20	9	23	32	22	62	12	15	5	4	200

TOTAL FG%	1st Half:	10-24 41.7%	2nd Half:	11-28 39.3%	Game:	40.4%	DEADB
3-Pt. FG%	1st Half:	2-6 33.3%	2nd Half:	4-11 36.4%	Game:	35.3%	REBS
F Throw %	1st Half:	12-17 70.6%	2nd Half:	2-3 66.7%	Game:	70.0%	3

Officials: Anthony Jordan, Mike Nance, Roger Ayers

Technical fouls: Kentucky — TEAM. Tennessee — None.

Attendance: 21,678

Score by Periods	1st	2nd	Total
Kentucky	28	37	65
Tennessee	34	28	62

John Calipari talked to Darius Miller and Marquis Teague in the first half in Knoxville.
David Perry | Lexington Herald-Leader

#14 MICHAEL KIDD-GILCHRIST

BY: JOHN CLAY | WILDCAT FEATURE

WHO'S CATS' EARLY MVP?

It's MKG

Quick question: Who has been the pre-Christmas Most Valuable Player on this Kentucky basketball team?

My vote goes to the player who is all about the fire, not the flash.

My vote goes to the player who plays like he just popped out of the toaster.

My vote goes to the player who always seems to grab the game by the horns.

And, as John Calipari said after Kentucky's 87-63 win over Loyola of Maryland on Thursday afternoon, the prayers of the Big Blue Nation should go for one Michael Kidd-Gilchrist, who scored 15 points and grabbed seven rebounds.

This, despite the fact that Kidd-Gilchrist's mother is in the hospital back home in New Jersey undergoing tests.

UK would not say the nature of the health problem, other than Calipari saying he hoped "that what we find out is all good."

Nor was Kidd-Gilchrist made available for post-game interviews, as well as his teammates so they could make a quicker getaway for Christmas break.

But then, Kidd-Gilchrist says more with his actions on the floor. Through these first 12 games, no Cat has been as consistent in his effort and his production.

"I'll be honest with you; he's dragging our team, which is great stuff," Calipari said Thursday. "He's doing it whether it's rebounding, scoring, making free throws, making threes when he has to."

Or starting the Breakfast Club; an idea that the freshman didn't even know he had hatched when he began working out early in the morning and eating breakfast before the morning practices.

Calipari liked the routine so much, the coach has all but tried to shame MKG's teammates into following.

"My job as a coach is to teach all these young people how to lead," Calipari said Thursday. "But as your season goes on, a couple of leaders will stand out amongst the group."

It's hard to lead, of course, when you are not doing what you are supposed to do on the floor. Kidd-Gilchrist has done that, and more.

Michael Kidd-Gilchrist showed off his jersey as No. 1 Kentucky defeated Tennessee 69-44 in Lexington.
Mark Cornelison | Lexington Herald-Leader

Thing is, he does it in a different way. He's not the best shooter on the team, or the best rebounder, or the best passer. Yet he does all three with amazing frequency and with admirable intensity.

It might not sound right to call him the ultimate garbage player, but Kidd-Gilchrist is exactly that in that he seems to snatch every loose ball, stick in every follow shot, plus play suffocating defense.

"In transition, if you give it to him ahead of the pack and it's him and one guy, he's scoring 99 percent of the time or he's going to get fouled," Calipari said.

This isn't to downgrade the early contributions of Kidd-Gilchrist's teammates, mind you.

Anthony Davis turned in his fifth double-double of the season, scoring 15 points and grabbing 11 rebounds. Marquis Teague's floor game is getting progressively better. Darius Miller is playing like a senior should.

Doron Lamb had produced five straight double-figure scoring games before being held to nine points - all in the first 14 minutes - by Loyola. And Kyle Wiltjer popped off the bench to score a career-high 24 points on Thursday.

"When we click and we come together and we're all playing aggressive and we're all bouncing and talking and all making easy plays, this stuff gets crazy," Calipari said. "We're not close to that right now."

MKG sure seems close to scary-good right now, which made it all the more odd Thursday when Loyola of Maryland coach Jimmy Patsos said that before the game he mistakenly believed the Greyhounds might have an advantage at MKG's position.

"I was wrong," said Patsos. "He's not flashy, he just drives the ball. ... He makes a lot of little plays, drove in, kicked it, got a rebound. Fifteen, seven and four assists. He was better than I thought."

On this Kentucky basketball team, Michael Kidd-Gilchrist has been the pre-Christmas MVP.■

Michael Kidd-Gilchrist went up against South Carolina's Lakeem Jackson in Rupp Arena.
David Perry | Lexington Herald-Leader

VS. ALABAMA

WILDCATS 77
CRIMSON TIDE 71

RUPP ARENA JANUARY 21, 2012

BY: JERRY TIPTON REGULAR SEASON

UK TIDE TURNERS

Miller clutch at foul line late in game

A two-way street named Resiliency went through Rupp Arena on Saturday.

Kentucky showed it could overcome truly foul shooting from the free-throw line, "merely" productive play from freshman star Anthony Davis and an opponent equipped to exacerbate Coach John Calipari's phobia about physical play.

Alabama bounced back from a disappointing home loss less than 48 hours earlier, refused to lose confidence in its perimeter shooting despite season-long discouragement and found itself inside the final 20 seconds with a chance to snap UK's nearly three-year home winning streak.

Ironically, Kentucky could credit free throws for its 77-71 victory.

Darius Miller made four of four in the final minute to ease the Cats to a 47th straight home victory. Kentucky, which made only 12 of its first 22 free throws, made eight of eight in the final minute. The Cats made 15 of their final 18, thereby compensating for not scoring a field goal in the final 6:57.

Asked to explain the rags-to-riches free-throw shooting, Calipari said, "I have no idea.

"I can't explain the 14 1-footers we missed in the first half either."

UK (19-1, 5-0 Southeastern Conference)

Coach John Calipari talked with guards Darius Miller (1) and Marquis Teague (25) during the Alabama game. *Mark Cornelison | Lexington Herald-Leader*

had more than a few of those shots around the basket because of Alabama's determination to contain Davis. UK's trademark lobs to the 6-foot-10 freshman were few.

"We watched him play," said JaMychal Green, who led the Tide with 22 points and 12 rebounds. "We saw a lot of lobs and dunks. We knew that's how he scores."

So Alabama (13-6, 2-3) kept a defender on Davis. Or as Calipari colorfully noted, "Somebody's hip was on him 24/7 until the game ended. As a matter of fact, they put a hip on him in the post-game handshake, too."

The attention to Davis made for open lanes to the basket once the Cats beat the on-ball defender. But still, UK made only 43.1 percent of its shots.

"Those are buckets we usually have," Davis said of the misses. "Like guaranteed."

Much like cross-state rival Auburn 10 days earlier, Alabama attacked Davis directly rather than let him domi-

Darius Miller hit a free throw with 14 seconds left as Kentucky defeated Alabama 77-71 in Rupp Arena.
Mark Cornelison | Lexington Herald-Leader

nate as a help-defender. Freshman Nick Jacobs complemented Green with nine points, his high for an SEC game.

"That was our No. 1 thing," Green said of the plan to make Davis play on-ball defense. "... Always go at his chest so he's not able to block shots."

Alabama Coach Anthony Grant cooled post-game enthusiasm for the plan by noting that Davis had 11 points, nine rebounds, four blocks and a career-high four steals.

"I think any coach in this league would take that," Grant said.

But for a "double-double machine," as teammate Doron Lamb called Davis, it was a relatively quiet game.

"One of the most physical teams I've played," Davis said of Alabama. "I know it's going to get worse."

Asked how he knew even more physical opponents awaited him, Davis said, "Other teams (are) just like that. There will be no games off. Vanderbilt (Festus Ezeli). Florida (Patric Young). Georgia (Marcus Thornton, Donte' Williams)."

Coming off a one-sided home loss to Vanderbilt on Thursday night, Alabama made 12 of its first 17 shots in the second half — led by point guard Trevor Releford's 6-for-6 perfection — to be within two with as little as 14 seconds left.

Kentucky led 37-32 at halftime. But a sense of dissatisfaction hung in the air. UK made only four of 11 first-half free throws, which was poorer accuracy than the Cats' three-point shooting (5-for-10).

Kentucky entered the game leading the SEC in free-throw accuracy (71.8 percent).

"We missed seven free throws and 14 1-footers in the first half," Calipari said. "We're lucky we were in the game."

Davis missed his first seven shots (the seventh being a lob dunk) and finished the game 2-for-10, a dramatic dip for a player ranked fourth nationally in accuracy (65.8 percent).

"Anthony was not the same guy," Calipari said.

Neither were Alabama's perimeter shooters. The Tide came into the game having made only 26.9 percent of their three-point shots. The official NCAA statistics stop at 27 percent. Or after 277 teams. Only nine Division I teams averaged fewer three-point baskets than Alabama's 3.9.

Yet the Tide made five of seven against UK.

"Teams will do that to us," said Calipari, who claimed to have predicted as much on his pre-game radio interview. "I imagine they'll come in and make every three, where that's one of the worst parts of their game. Which they did."■

Anthony Davis and Terrence Jones combined to stop Alabama forward Tony Mitchell.
Mark Cornelison | Lexington Herald-Leader

BOX SCORE

ALABAMA

## Player Name	TOT-FG FG-FGA	3-PT FG-FGA	FT-FTA	REBOUNDS OF	DE	TOT	PF	TP	A	TO	BLK	S	MIN
01 Green, Jamychal..... f	8-13	0-0	6-8	4	8	12	3	22	0	3	1	0	36
05 Mitchell, Tony...... f	2-9	1-1	1-3	3	1	4	5	6	0	2	1	1	20
03 Lacey, Trevor....... g	4-7	2-4	0-0	0	5	5	2	10	5	3	0	0	35
12 Releford, Trevor.... g	6-8	2-2	3-5	1	2	3	3	17	3	0	0	2	36
20 Randolph, Levi...... g	0-1	0-0	0-0	0	1	1	3	0	1	1	0	0	14
02 Hankerson, Charles..	0-1	0-0	0-0	0	0	0	1	0	0	0	0	0	0+
14 Gueye, Moussa.......	0-0	0-0	3-4	0	2	2	3	3	0	2	0	0	5
15 Jacobs, Nick........	4-10	0-0	1-1	1	2	3	2	9	0	2	0	0	28
22 Steele, Andrew......	0-1	0-0	4-4	0	2	2	5	4	2	1	0	0	26
TEAM................				1	2	3							
Totals..............	24-50	5-7	18-25	10	25	35	27	71	11	14	2	3	200

TOTAL FG%	1st Half:	11-30 36.7%	2nd Half:	13-20 65.0%	Game:	48.0%	DEADB
3-Pt. FG%	1st Half:	3-4 75.0%	2nd Half:	2-3 66.7%	Game:	71.4%	REBS
F Throw %	1st Half:	7-10 70.0%	2nd Half:	11-15 73.3%	Game:	72.0%	3

KENTUCKY

## Player Name	TOT-FG FG-FGA	3-PT FG-FGA	FT-FTA	REBOUNDS OF	DE	TOT	PF	TP	A	TO	BLK	S	MIN
03 Jones, Terrence..... f	4-7	1-2	6-12	3	3	6	4	15	1	2	2	1	32
14 Kidd-Gilchrist, M... f	4-7	0-1	5-7	1	5	6	5	13	1	0	1	2	23
23 Davis, Anthony...... f	2-10	0-0	7-9	6	3	9	2	11	0	0	4	4	39
01 Miller, Darius...... g	2-5	2-4	5-6	1	1	2	2	11	4	2	1	2	29
25 Teague, Marquis..... g	4-11	0-1	2-4	1	1	2	2	10	1	3	0	0	38
20 Lamb, Doron.........	5-8	2-3	2-2	0	4	4	3	14	2	1	0	0	33
33 Wiltjer, Kyle.......	1-3	1-3	0-0	0	1	1	0	3	0	0	1	0	6
TEAM................				1		1							
Totals..............	22-51	6-14	27-40	13	18	31	18	77	9	8	9	9	200

TOTAL FG%	1st Half:	14-31 45.2%	2nd Half:	8-20 40.0%	Game:	43.1%	DEADB
3-Pt. FG%	1st Half:	5-10 50.0%	2nd Half:	1-4 25.0%	Game:	42.9%	REBS
F Throw %	1st Half:	4-11 36.4%	2nd Half:	23-29 79.3%	Game:	67.5%	4,2

Officials: Doug Shows, Mike Nance, Doug Sirmons

Technical fouls: Alabama — None. Kentucky — None.

Attendance: 24,246

Score by Periods	1st	2nd	Total
Alabama	32	39	71
Kentucky	37	40	77

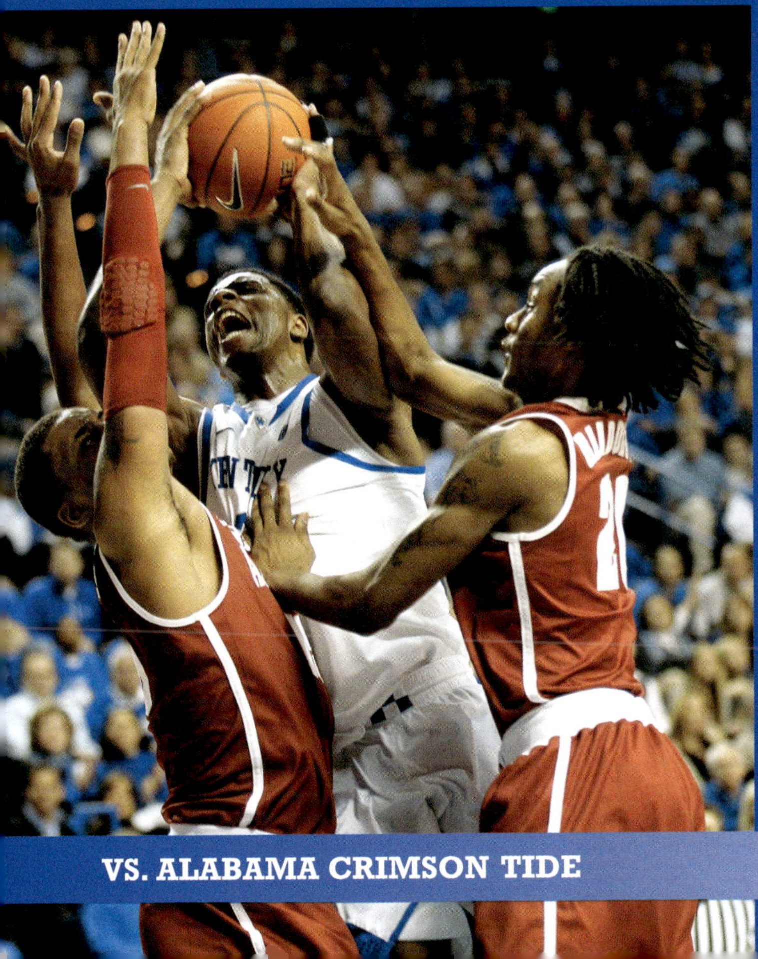

Above: Anthony Davis pulled down one of his 9 rebounds as No. 2 Kentucky defeated Alabama 77-71.
Mark Cornelison | Lexington Herald-Leader

Left: Terrence Jones was sandwiched by Alabama forward Nick Jacobs, left, and guard Levi Randolph as he drove to the basket in the second half against Alabama.
David Perry | Lexington Herald-Leader

AT VANDERBILT

WILDCATS 69
COMMODORES 63

MEMORIAL GYM FEBRUARY 11, 2012

BY: JOHN CLAY REGULAR SEASON

VANDY MAKES CATS EARN IT

Game wasn't comfortable, but it was impressive

Those easy-as-you-please 20-point blowouts over various opponents might be good for the collective blood pressure of the forever fretting Big Blue Nation.

But give me Kentucky's 69-63 white-knuckler of a win over Vanderbilt on Saturday night at an energized Memorial Gymnasium.

This victory was much more impressive.

And it had nothing to do with this being ESPN's GameDay or some UK fans' misguided attempts to wreck it, or the crabby Digger Phelps, or the benches on the baseline, or any of that off-the-floor stuff.

Here's what was impressive: Finally, Kentucky had to take a punch in the second half from a good team playing on the good team's home floor.

The Cats took the punch, and punched right back, and landed the knockout blow.

After all, No. 1 Kentucky all but cruised in the first 20 minutes of the marquee matchup, up 36-23 at the break.

Marquis Teague was outstanding, the freshman point guard controlling the tempo, driving past Vandy point guard Brad Tinsley to make buckets at the basket, or passing for teammates' buckets at the basket.

Terrence Jones wasn't bad either. The sophomore scored 14 points and grabbed five rebounds in the first 20 minutes.

"He took his game from 20 feet and condensed it down to 6," said UK Coach John Calipari. "And he was a man."

But the Cats knew it wasn't over.

Terrence Jones put in a shot over Vanderbilt forward Lance Goulbourne. *Mark Cornelison | Lexington Herald-Leader*

Doron Lamb (20) drove the lane for a basket as No. 1 Kentucky played Vanderbilt on Feb. 9 in Nashville.
Mark Cornelison | Lexington Herald-Leader

"This is their home floor," said center Anthony Davis. "We knew they would make a run."

And indeed Kevin Stallings' team roared back. The 'Dores shooters got going. (They would end up 8-for-21 from three.) The crowd got behind them. And Vandy tied it at 48, then went ahead 53-51 on a Brad Tinsley basket.

When Festus Ezeli scored inside at the 8:42 mark, the Commodores led 55-51.

For Calipari, it was a you-asked-for-it-you-got-it moment. Even after his team's 20-point win over visiting Florida on Tuesday, the Kentucky coach said he would truly find out about his team when the opponent went crazy, was throwing in threes, making plays, putting the Cats' backs to the wall.

Calipari said he wanted to see how his team would respond.

It responded — not once, but twice.

First, the Cats went on a 10-2 run to take a 61-57 lead at the six-minute mark.

But Vandy battled back and stuck a nose in front 63-61 on another Tinsley basket at the 4:10 mark.

Here's the thing: The Commodores would not score again.

Not one point.

On the offensive end, the visitors scored the game's final eight points, despite missing a boatload of free throws.

On the defensive end, Kentucky's best end, the Cats went into full lock-down mode. The best defensive team in the nation, via field goal percentage defense, held the Commodores without a point over the final 4:10.

"We're a good defensive team," said Calipari.

Vanderbilt missed nine shots. The 'Dores missed three-pointers. The 'Dores missed twos. On one possession, Vandy forward Jeffery Taylor had his three-pointer from the top of the key deflected to where it hit teammate Ezeli in the back of the head. Kentucky got the loose ball.

In the end, Kentucky got the win, its 17th straight, and 25th out of 26 this year. The Cats are now 11-0 in the SEC.

The latter victories had been closer to walkovers — on the road last Saturday at South Carolina by 34, then at home on Tuesday against Florida by 20.

Said Calipari, with a glimmer in his eye, "I'd prefer to be up 23."

Yes, the blowouts are nice. But the ones that come in the clutch against a good team on the road, the ones that are earned, those are much better.

And more impressive.■

Anthony Davis dunked for two of his 15 points, to go with 7 blocks, against Vanderbilt.
Mark Cornelison | Lexington Herald-Leader

BOX SCORE

KENTUCKY

## Player Name	TOT-FG FG-FGA	3-PT FG-FGA	FT-FTA	REBOUNDS OF	REBOUNDS DE	REBOUNDS TOT	PF	TP	A	TO	BLK	S	MIN
03 Jones, Terrence..... f	6-10	0-0	2-3	4	5	9	3	14	0	0	4	2	30
14 Kidd-Gilchrist, M... f	1-4	0-1	2-3	0	7	7	3	4	1	3	1	1	30
23 Davis, Anthony...... f	6-12	0-0	3-3	4	4	8	3	15	0	1	7	0	39
20 Lamb, Doron......... g	6-13	2-7	2-3	0	2	2	2	16	1	1	0	1	37
25 Teague, Marquis..... g	6-12	0-3	1-3	1	3	4	0	13	8	1	0	0	37
01 Miller, Darius......	2-5	1-2	0-0	0	2	2	4	5	2	0	0	0	15
33 Wiltjer, Kyle.......	1-2	0-1	0-0	0	1	1	1	2	0	0	0	0	12
TEAM................				1	1	2							
Totals.............	28-58	3-14	10-15	10	25	35	16	69	12	6	12	4	200

TOTAL FG%	1st Half:	16-30 53.3%	2nd Half:	12-28 42.9%	Game:	48.3%	DEADB
3-Pt. FG%	1st Half:	0-4 0.0%	2nd Half:	3-10 30.0%	Game:	21.4%	REBS
F Throw %	1st Half:	4-6 66.7%	2nd Half:	6-9 66.7%	Game:	66.7%	4

VANDERBILT

## Player Name	TOT-FG FG-FGA	3-PT FG-FGA	FT-FTA	REBOUNDS OF	REBOUNDS DE	REBOUNDS TOT	PF	TP	A	TO	BLK	S	MIN
05 GOULBOURNE, Lance... f	1-9	0-2	1-2	5	3	8	1	3	3	1	0	1	31
44 TAYLOR, Jeffery..... f	5-11	2-5	1-1	3	6	9	5	13	4	2	0	0	35
03 EZELI, Festus....... c	5-12	0-0	3-6	2	4	6	3	13	0	3	2	0	27
01 TINSLEY, Brad....... g	5-12	3-5	0-0	1	4	5	2	13	4	3	1	1	34
23 JENKINS, John....... g	5-14	3-9	2-3	0	2	2	1	15	0	1	0	2	39
02 JOHNSON, Kedren.....	0-1	0-0	0-0	0	0	0	1	0	2	0	0	0	6
24 PARKER, Dai-Jon.....	0-0	0-0	0-0	1	0	1	0	0	0	0	0	0	6
33 TCHIENGANG, Steve...	2-4	0-0	2-2	0	0	0	1	6	0	0	0	0	13
45 ODOM, Rod...........	0-0	0-0	0-0	0	0	0	1	0	1	0	1	0	9
TEAM................				5	2	7							
Totals.............	23-63	8-21	9-14	17	21	38	15	63	14	10	4	4	200

TOTAL FG%	1st Half:	8-29 27.6%	2nd Half:	15-34 44.1%	Game:	36.5%	DEADB
3-Pt. FG%	1st Half:	3-9 33.3%	2nd Half:	5-12 41.7%	Game:	38.1%	REBS
F Throw %	1st Half:	4-8 50.0%	2nd Half:	5-6 83.3%	Game:	64.3%	3

Officials: Tony Greene, Joe Lindsay, Gary Maxwell

Technical fouls: Kentucky — None. Vanderbilt — None.

Attendance: 14,316

Score by Periods	1st	2nd	Total
Kentucky	36	33	69
Vanderbilt	23	40	63

Above: Anthony Davis was all smiles as he came down the floor after one of his 7 blocks. *Mark Cornelison | Lexington Herald-Leader*

Far Left: Terrence Jones (3) blocked the shot of Vanderbilt's Lance Goulbourne, as Anthony Davis closed in from behind. *Mark Cornelison | Lexington Herald-Leader*

Left: Anthony Davis blocked the shot of Vanderbilt center Festus Ezeli for one of his 7 blocks in the game. *Mark Cornelison | Lexington Herald-Leader*

#20 DORON LAMB

BY: JOHN CLAY

WILDCAT FEATURE

LAMB LIVING UP TO CAL'S PROPHETIC PRAISE

Over the summer, coach proclaimed player as UK's best

Back in the summer, John Calipari raised a few eyebrows when he proclaimed Doron Lamb as Kentucky's best player.

This, like many other utterances from the active mind of the UK coach, required a Calipari clarification.

Upon explanation, he noted the 6-foot-4 guard from New York wasn't his tallest, or his fastest, or his strongest. Lamb was, however, his most complete player.

But now, through three games of the 2011-12 college basketball season, no explanation necessary.

Back home Tuesday night in his Big Apple, the King of Queens scored 17 points and dished four assists as second-ranked Kentucky took care of No. 12 Kansas in the Champions Classic at Madison Square Garden.

Then Saturday, here among the ramblers and gamblers at the Mohegan Sun Casino — "Just go all the way past the slot machines and turn left," answered a casino worker when asked where someone might pick up media credentials — Lamb scored a game-high 26 points as the Cats pummeled Penn State 85-47 in the semifinals of the Hall of Fame Tip-Off Tournament.

"Why is Doron playing so well?" Calipari rhetorically asked afterward. "His motor's going."

"I'm glad he's not saying I don't have a motor anymore," said Lamb later.

His is in top gear. Lamb has made 18 of 33 field goals, nine of 16 three-pointers and 13 of 15 free throws. Moreover, he has 11 assists compared to just two turnovers.

"He's not playing a casual game, like he did last year at times," Calipari said. "Now he's got a motor running, and you see him out there, and you say, 'Man is he playing!' "

Doron Lamb smiled after the clock ran out with Kentucky leading Florida 74-71 in the SEC tournament in New Orleans. *Pablo Alcalá | Lexington Herald-Leader*

Off the court, Lamb is a casual guy, laid back and funny with a shy smile. Example: In the post-game locker room, the sophomore was asked about his new 2011-12 hairstyle.

"I'm just going to keep my hair a little nappy-fro this year," he said. "Last year, I had no time for getting haircuts and my hair was all messed up all the time. I'm just going to keep it nappy, it's better like this."

Nappy-fro?

"It's called 'Nappy Boy,'" he said with a smile.

Hairstyles aside, what has it been like coming back to your old stomping grounds?

"It was an honor to come back home in front of my family and friends and play in the Garden my second time," he said. "As a team, we all played great. I had fun out there in New York, off the court and on the court."

The team spent a rainy Wednesday in New York before continuing to Connecticut on Thursday. They toured ESPN's campus, even practiced in the World Wide Leader's Bristol gym.

Then Saturday, while Calipari admitted to be worried about the noon tip-off, the Cats took care of the Nittany Lions in short order, up 47-15 at the half.

Lamb hit the jackpot with 17 first-half points. His 26 points ranked second on his career scoring list to the 32 he rained down on Winthrop last season.

"Just as coach said, my motor is getting better," Lamb said. "I've been working out with (assistant coach) Kenny Payne before practice and off days, getting a lot of conditioning in on the treadmill. Just working on my ball-handling and my skills, and it's paying off on the court."

"He only had one turnover," Calipari said. "He's not our fastest. He doesn't jump the highest. He's not the longest. He's not the tallest. He just has a feel for the game."

Coming out of prep school wasn't Lamb known as primarily a shooter?

"In my opinion, he's the best two-point shooter in college basketball," Calipari said. "He's a good three-point shooter. But if he gets something from 15 to 17 feet, he's one of those guys, he makes that shot. I don't know if there's anybody better in college basketball."

And when it comes to choosing Kentucky's best all-around player, Cal is being proven once again correct.

Keep those 'brows down.■

Doron Lamb against Georgia in Athens, Ga. *David Perry | Lexington Herald-Leader*

AT MISSISSIPPI STATE

WILDCATS 73
BULLDOGS 64

HUMPHREY COLISEUM **FEBRUARY 21, 2012**

BY: JERRY TIPTON REGULAR SEASON

CATS DEFLATE STATE

UK erases 13-point halftime deficit, clinches share of SEC

The largest halftime deficit in more than a year in a game played under "white-out" conditions could not prevent No. 1 Kentucky from seeing its way to victory Tuesday night.

Led by Michael Kidd-Gilchrist, UK rallied to beat Mississippi State 73-64.

The Cats trailed by 13 at halftime.

"We should have been down 20 the way we played and the way they played," UK Coach John Calipari said. "I told them at halftime, 'This isn't all bad. Let's show what we're made of.' "

Then Calipari added, facetiously, "Everybody rooting for us. Let's make them angry."

With Kidd-Gilchrist stifling Dee Bost, UK rode a 15-2 run down the stretch to its 27th victory in 28 games.

Bost, who torched UK for 16 first-half points, made only one of six second-half shots and finished with 21. But his impact diminished greatly as the Cats chipped away.

"I was thinking of starting the game that way," Calipari said of Kidd-Gilchrist on Bost. "Obviously, I made a mistake not starting that way. ... Dee carried them."

Kentucky, which clinched at least a share of the Southeastern Conference championship (13-0), caught a break when State's Rodney Hood sprained a knee late in the half.

Gone went a three-point shooter and, State Coach Rick Stansbury added, a defender to put on Kidd-Gilchrist at small forward. Instead, the smaller Brian Bryant took the role.

Above: Darius Miller made a 3-pointer to put UK ahead 71-64 against Mississippi State. UK won 73-64. *Charles Bertram | Lexington Herald-Leader*

Right: Michael Kidd-Gilchrist blocked a shot by Mississippi State's Brian Bryant in the first half. *Charles Bertram | Lexington Herald-Leader*

KIDD-GILCHRIST
14
BRYANT
22
LAMB
20

Anthony Davis, Terrence Jones and Michael Kidd-Gilchrist swarmed Mississippi State's Arnett Moultrie in the second half.
Charles Bertram | Lexington Herald-Leader

"Huge, huge, huge blow," Stansbury said. "... With our lack of depth, it's huge for us. Now we got to play a guy who can't physically guard Gilchrist."

Mississippi State fell to 19-9 overall and 6-7 in the SEC.

Kidd-Gilchrist led UK with 18 points. Anthony Davis added 13. Darius Miller, who didn't score until less than eight minutes remained, added 12. His points were a big part of a 20-4 Kentucky run to finish the game.

"Darius Miller is the fiber that holds that whole team together," Stansbury said. "... He's the guy they look to when the game gets out of line."

A sellout crowd, largely dressed in white, rocked the Humphrey Coliseum in the first half, then quietly exited in the final minute.

Kentucky trailed 41-28 at halftime. Not only did that mark UK's largest halftime deficit of the season, but it was their biggest since falling behind Connecticut 50-29 on Maui last season.

Until this game, the Cats had not trailed by double digits all season, the largest previous deficit being 34-25 against North Carolina.

Yet State jumped ahead 12-2 at the 14:42 mark. Thereafter, Kentucky trailed by double digits for all but 5:57 the rest of the half. The deficit grew to as much as 13 points when Bost hit one of his two first-half three-pointers with 4:26 left.

Another three-pointer, this time by Jalen Steele, set the halftime score with 41.8 seconds left. State, which made only five of 22 three-pointers in last weekend's loss at Auburn, hit six of 11 in the first half. Bost, who made only two of nine shots at Auburn, had 16 first-half points.

Overall, the Bulldogs shot a healthy 48.3 percent (14-for-29) while UK struggled. Settling for too many perimeter jumpers, the Cats made one of their first 11 shots in falling behind from the start. UK made just five of its first 18 shots en route to a 38.7 percent shooting half.

A halftime deficit was something new for Kentucky, which led at the half in its last nine games, six times by 12 or more points.

State had won 17 of 19 games in which it led at halftime this season.

With Kidd-Gilchrist guarding Bost, Kentucky's defense led a rally to open the second half. State scored only one basket in the first four minutes.

Meanwhile, UK chipped away, closing within four, 43-39, on two Davis free throws with 16:04 left. That marked the smallest UK deficit since trailing 5-2.

A technical foul on Davis for hanging on the rim after a steal and a driving dunk stalled Kentucky's rally momentarily.

Bost made both technical free throws to give State a 47-41 lead with 13:51 left.

UK closed to within two, 55-53 with just more than seven minutes to go. But Moultrie slammed home a putback, then stared at Terrence Jones.

After Lamb missed a quick-trigger three, Bost hit a three-pointer to put State ahead 60-53, prompting a UK timeout with 6:27 left. It was Bost's first basket of the second half.

Miller, who did not score in the game's first 32 minutes, scored nine points in less than three minutes to bring the Cats within one, 62-61.

Kentucky took its first lead at the 4:06 mark. Kidd-Gilchrist rebounded his own miss and scored to put the Cats ahead 63-62.■

BOX SCORE

KENTUCKY

## Player Name	TOT-FG FG-FGA	3-PT FG-FGA	FT-FTA	REBOUNDS OF	DE	TOT	PF	TP	A	TO	BLK	S	MIN
03 Jones, Terrence..... f	5-12	0-1	1-3	5	1	6	3	11	1	2	1	1	33
14 Kidd-Gilchrist, M... f	7-12	0-1	4-5	1	9	10	0	18	1	1	2	2	36
23 Davis, Anthony...... f	4-9	0-2	5-6	3	8	11	1	13	1	1	2	2	38
20 Lamb, Doron......... g	3-9	1-3	4-4	0	1	1	0	11	2	0	0	1	33
25 Teague, Marquis..... g	3-8	2-3	0-0	0	2	2	4	8	2	3	0	0	23
01 Miller, Darius......	3-7	3-6	3-3	0	3	3	2	12	3	0	0	1	31
30 Vargas, Eloy........	0-0	0-0	0-0	0	0	0	0	0	0	0	0	0	2
33 Wiltjer, Kyle.......	0-0	0-0	0-0	0	0	0	0	0	0	1	0	0	4
TEAM...............				2	1	3				1			
Totals.............	25-57	6-16	17-21	11	25	36	10	73	10	9	5	7	200

TOTAL FG%	1st Half: 12-31 38.7%	2nd Half: 13-26 50.0%	Game:	43.9%	DEADB
3-Pt. FG%	1st Half: 2-6 33.3%	2nd Half: 4-10 40.0%	Game:	37.5%	REBS
F Throw %	1st Half: 2-4 50.0%	2nd Half: 15-17 88.2%	Game:	81.0%	2

MISSISSIPPI STATE

## Player Name	TOT-FG FG-FGA	3-PT FG-FGA	FT-FTA	REBOUNDS OF	DE	TOT	PF	TP	A	TO	BLK	S	MIN
01 Renardo Sidney...... f	1-6	1-2	0-2	0	1	1	4	3	1	0	0	1	22
23 Arnett Moultrie..... f	6-10	0-1	1-1	3	8	11	2	13	2	3	2	0	39
03 Dee Bost............ g	5-15	3-6	8-8	0	2	2	4	21	7	3	0	4	38
04 Rodney Hood......... g	2-6	2-4	0-0	1	1	2	1	6	0	1	0	0	12
22 Brian Bryant........ g	3-6	0-0	0-2	0	5	5	1	6	2	1	1	0	35
00 Jalen Steele........	4-8	3-7	2-2	0	1	1	2	13	1	2	0	0	33
10 Shaun Smith.........	0-0	0-0	0-0	0	0	0	0	0	0	0	0	0	0+
30 Wendell Lewis.......	1-3	0-0	0-0	1	2	3	3	2	0	1	1	0	19
33 DeVille Smith.......	0-0	0-0	0-0	1	0	1	0	0	0	1	0	0	2
TEAM...............				3	3	6							
Totals.............	22-54	9-20	11-15	9	23	32	17	64	13	12	4	5	200

TOTAL FG%	1st Half: 14-29 48.3%	2nd Half: 8-25 32.0%	Game:	40.7%	DEADB
3-Pt. FG%	1st Half: 6-12 50.0%	2nd Half: 3-8 37.5%	Game:	45.0%	REBS
F Throw %	1st Half: 7-7 100 %	2nd Half: 4-8 50.0%	Game:	73.3%	2

Officials: Ted Valentine, Doug Shows, Bert Smith

Technical fouls: Kentucky — Teague, Marquis; Davis, Anthony.
Mississippi State — Arnett Moultrie.

Attendance: 10,213

Score by Periods	1st	2nd	Total
Kentucky	28	45	73
Mississippi State	41	23	64

Michael Kidd- Gilchrist, left, and Darius Miller battled Mississippi State's Arnett Moultrie for a rebound in UK's 73-64 win. *Charles Bertram | Lexington Herald-Leader*

AT FLORIDA

WILDCATS	74
GATORS	59

STEPHEN C. O'CONNELL CENTER MARCH 4, 2012

BY: JERRY TIPTON REGULAR SEASON

SWEEP SIXTEEN

Road win caps Cats' perfect season in SEC

If a rare bit of history can be made in a wholly predictable way, Kentucky did it Sunday. UK used its by-now routine knack for clutch play and an unmistakable superiority to beat back Florida 74-59.

The victory — accompanied by the customary sound track (the UK fans here chanted "Go, Big Blue" several times) — enabled Kentucky to go where few have tread: The Cats became only the third team since 1956 to go unbeaten in Southeastern Conference play and, in a program for which historic achievement remains largely out of reach, became the first UK team to win 30 games in a regular season.

"If somebody's going to beat that, they'll have to win 31," Coach John Calipari said. "Which is all of them."

Kentucky trailed only once. When Florida reduced a 16-point first-half lead to two barely three minutes into the second half, the Cats rose to the challenge.

"If you break down against them, you're going to pay," Florida Coach Billy Donovan said in tribute to the Cats. "But they also have an ability to to make (clutch) shots. When you do guard them the way you want them guarded, they can still make the shot."

Florida reset the stage for another example of UK resolve by closing within two at 46-44. That marked UK's smallest lead since 15-14. More than 16 minutes remained.

After calling a timeout with 16:29 left, Calipari inserted Darius Miller, UK's Mr. Clutch in both Vanderbilt games and at Mississippi State.

The move paid off 22 seconds later as Miller swished a pull-up jumper despite being bumped as he rose.

With Florida lurking at 51-44, freshman big man Anthony Davis swished a three-pointer from the top

Anthony Davis made the "3 goggles" sign after making a 3-pointer in the second half against Florida.
Charles Bertram | Lexington Herald-Leader

Darius Miller hit a short floating jumper in the second half against Florida. *Charles Bertram | Lexington Herald-Leader*

of the key. Until Thursday against Georgia, he hadn't made a shot from beyond the arc, not that he couldn't.

"I didn't really need to," he said. "The way teams are playing me, backing off, it leaves me open. Coach Cal said to put up shots."

Davis, who finished with 22 points, 12 rebounds and six blocks, responded again when Florida closed within four, 57-53. He swooped into the lane and tossed in a — where's that been? — left-handed baby hook.

Florida (22-9, 10-6 SEC) persisted. But with UK nursing a 61-55 lead, Terrence Jones swished a three-pointer. He hadn't made a trey since Jan. 21 against Alabama. Maybe, like Davis, he was saving it for when it was needed.

As if serving an appetizer for what was to come, Jones appeared to turn the wrong way and then shoot a 10-footer across his body. It rattled in to give the Cats a 46-40 lead.

Meanwhile, Florida went scoreless for more than four minutes after closing within two, 46-44.

Terrence Jones blocked a shot by Florida's Bradley Beal in the first half. *Charles Bertram | Lexington Herald-Leader*

UK improved to 30-1 overall and 16-0 in the SEC. Since 1956, the only two teams to win every league game were Kentucky in 1995-96 and 2002-03.

Donovan likened this UK team to the latter.

Noting the lead role played by Chuck Hayes (incidentally, only the fifth-leading scorer) in 2002-03, the Florida coach said of the current Cats, "These guys are equally effective, but so much more gifted and talented than Hayes.

"He was the whole key when you're talking of making timely plays. They have several guys who can make timely plays."

Kentucky trailed for all of 25 seconds, which reminded anyone still needing reminding which team clearly is the SEC's best this season.

With Jones exploiting his matchup with Erik Murphy, Kentucky led by as much as 16 points before settling for a 40-32 lead at intermission. Jones scored 14 of his 19 in the first half.

"I thought it was a (favorable) matchup," Calipari said. "I told him, 'Terrence, you're one of the top five players in the country; play that way.' "

The UK lead reached its zenith — 38-22 with 4:10 left — when Jones hit a putback of Marquis Teague's quasi lob/shot that bounced off the rim.

"He came out very strong," Davis said of Jones. "If Terrence plays like that, I think it'll be very hard for anybody to beat us."

And if Jones doesn't play like that, well, Kentucky will still be hard to beat.

"This team has a will to win," Calipari said, repeating an observation he's made on several occasions this season. "I told them, 'If it's close, I feel good about it.' This team wants to win."

Even a relatively meaningless game with the SEC championship (and, surely a No. 1 seed in the NCAA Tournament) secured could not dull that will.

"We play to win," Calipari said. "We're not playing not to lose. That was my message: Go have pride and play."■

BOX SCORE

KENTUCKY

## Player Name	TOT-FG FG-FGA	3-PT FG-FGA	FT-FTA	REBOUNDS OF	DE	TOT	PF	TP	A	TO	BLK	S	MIN
03 Jones, Terrence..... f	9-13	1-1	0-1	2	2	4	1	19	1	0	3	2	36
14 Kidd-Gilchrist, M... f	3-7	0-1	1-2	4	4	8	2	7	4	2	0	2	36
23 Davis, Anthony...... f	9-13	1-2	3-4	3	9	12	1	22	0	1	6	0	36
20 Lamb, Doron......... g	2-7	1-3	0-0	0	1	1	2	5	1	0	0	0	34
25 Teague, Marquis..... g	4-9	1-2	3-4	0	2	2	3	12	4	1	0	1	33
01 Miller, Darius......	3-7	0-2	0-0	0	1	1	0	6	0	2	0	2	17
33 Wiltjer, Kyle.......	1-3	1-1	0-0	1	1	2	0	3	1	0	0	0	8
TEAM................				1	5	6							
Totals.............	31-59	5-12	7-11	11	25	36	9	74	11	6	9	7	200

TOTAL FG%	1st Half:	19-35 54.3%	2nd Half:	12-24 50.0%	Game: 52.5%	DEADB
3-Pt. FG%	1st Half:	2-6 33.3%	2nd Half:	3-6 50.0%	Game: 41.7%	REBS
F Throw %	1st Half:	0-1 0.0%	2nd Half:	7-10 70.0%	Game: 63.6%	0

FLORIDA

## Player Name	TOT-FG FG-FGA	3-PT FG-FGA	FT-FTA	REBOUNDS OF	DE	TOT	PF	TP	A	TO	BLK	S	MIN
33 Murphy, Erik........ f	4-9	2-5	4-4	2	6	8	1	14	2	1	0	0	36
04 Young, Patric....... c	10-15	0-0	1-1	5	4	9	1	21	0	0	0	0	35
05 Wilbekin, Scottie... g	0-0	0-0	0-0	0	1	1	2	0	1	1	1	0	22
11 Walker, Erving...... g	3-11	2-7	0-0	0	1	1	3	8	5	3	0	0	36
23 Beal, Bradley....... g	1-10	1-5	2-2	1	6	7	3	5	4	1	1	2	36
01 Boynton, Kenny......	2-8	1-5	2-2	0	1	1	0	7	2	0	0	1	25
03 Rosario, Mike.......	1-2	0-0	2-2	0	1	1	0	4	0	1	0	0	7
24 Prather, Casey......	0-0	0-0	0-0	0	0	0	0	0	0	0	0	0	3
TEAM................				1	1	2							
Totals.............	21-55	6-22	11-11	9	21	30	10	59	14	7	2	3	200

TOTAL FG%	1st Half:	12-28 42.9%	2nd Half:	9-27 33.3%	Game: 38.2%	DEADB
3-Pt. FG%	1st Half:	4-11 36.4%	2nd Half:	2-11 18.2%	Game: 27.3%	REBS
F Throw %	1st Half:	4-4 100 %	2nd Half:	7-7 100 %	Game: 100 %	0

Officials: Tony Greene, Doug Shows, Doug Sirmons

Technical fouls: Kentucky — None. Florida — None.

Attendance: 12,113

Score by Periods	1st	2nd	Total
Kentucky	40	34	74
Florida	32	27	59

Above: Marquis Teague looked to pass the ball on a drive around Florida's Patric Young and Erik Murphy. *Charles Bertram | Lexington Herald-Leader*

Left: Terrence Jones and Florida's Mike Rosario scrambled for a loose ball in the first half. *Charles Bertram | Lexington Herald-Leader*

#23 ANTHONY DAVIS

BY: JOHN CLAY

WILDCAT FEATURE

DAVIS' LEGACY: OH MY, NOT OH ME

A scene-stealer despite himself

In Gainesville on Sunday, once Kentucky had finished off its perfect SEC regular season, Anthony Davis, sporting a Chicago Cubs toboggan hat, was in a hallway of the O'Dome talking to the media.

Someone asked the 6-foot-10 freshman center about his making a three-pointer for the second straight game and about his perfect lead pass on a fast break.

Had he possessed those parts of his game all along, or were they new.

Davis said that he had them all along.

Then why didn't you show them?

"I didn't need to," he said.

In fact, said it as simply as that. He didn't say it in a boastful way. He didn't say it in a regretful way. He didn't say it to make any particular point, other than this: he has done whatever his team needed him to do.

On Tuesday, the rewards for such a distinct combination of talent and attitude began to flow in to the Craft Center.

First, the Sporting News announced it had chosen Davis as its National Player of the Year. Then later in the day, the SEC announced that the Chicago native had been chosen as its SEC Player of the Year.

Unfortunately, Davis was not there to comment on his individual bounty. He was back home on the sad occasion of a death in the family.

But we have been around him long enough to know what he most likely would have said, and not said.

He would have given thanks. He would have deflected attention to his teammates. He would have emitted a perhaps subtle, but no doubt discernible, feeling of pride.

Here is our reaction: If Anthony Davis is this good as a freshman, how extraordinarily good could he be down the road?

"When he made the right hook," said John Calipari on Tuesday, acting out the shot Davis made against the Gators, but with a mischievous grin and a twinkle in his eye, "and then we made the right hook ... I mean I had to go back to the TV copy because the guy on TV (Steve Kerr) said, 'Oh, my!' "

Anthony Davis dunked over Loyola's Jordan Latham in Rupp Arena. *Charles Bertram | Lexington Herald-Leader*

Kentucky fans have said, "Oh, my!" a lot this year, whether it be after a blocked shot by Davis, or a lob dunk by Davis, or, of late, a perimeter jumper by Davis.

Yet it never appears that Davis says that about himself, not on the floor. He doesn't pose or preen. He produces.

"He's very mature," said Florida Coach Billy Donovan on Sunday. "And that's rare."

"He's just getting better and better and better," said Calipari on Tuesday. "He doesn't say anything, doesn't shoot a whole lot of balls."

That has been Calipari's stump speech in favor of Davis for the big hardware — the Wooden Award, for example, which will be awarded after the Final Four.

Calipari's current line has been that Davis will end up taking 200 fewer shots than other contenders, most notably Kansas' outstanding forward Thomas Robinson.

In fact, Kansas Coach Bill Self argued on Robinson's behalf that the Jayhawk has had to carry more of the load, that his offense is predicated more on working the ball to the post than is Calipari's attack.

"Could you imagine if we went at Davis every possession?" said the coach Tuesday. "Could you imagine if he shot 22 times a game? ... Could you imagine if he played that way, how good he would be?

"Can you imagine the shots he would take, the threes he would have taken well before? The behind-the-back dribbles that you would have seen out of a kid 6-foot-11? You'll see it. You're just probably not going to see it (here)."

That's OK with Davis. He's not a scene-stealer. Make no mistake, he is determined. He is fearless. But he is also unselfish.

Donovan said Monday that the Kentucky players "just seemed consumed with winning, that's it. ... That's very impressive."

That's your Player of the Year.■

Anthony Davis attempted a dunk against Vanderbilt's Festus Ezeli in the second half of the SEC tournament championship in New Orleans. *Pablo Alcalá | Lexington Herald-Leader*

VS. LSU

WILDCATS	60
TIGERS	51

NEW ORLEANS — MARCH 9, 2012

BY: JERRY TIPTON — SEC TOURNAMENT: GAME 1

THE BIG UNEASY

Jones saves his best for Tigers as Cats move on

The Big Easy was anything but for Kentucky in its Southeastern Conference Tournament opening game Friday.

But despite the potentially knockout combination of its own turnover-plagued performance and LSU's competitive zeal, UK prevailed 60-51 in the New Orleans Arena.

Terrence Jones, the hero when the teams played in Baton Rouge, La., in late January, again loomed large. His nine straight points early in the second half gave Kentucky a lead to nurse to the finish line.

"For whatever reason, he likes us," said LSU Coach Trent Johnson, who memorably declared the Cats the regular-season champs if Jones could replicate his 27-point, nine-rebound, three-block performance in Baton Rouge.

A second double-double of the season (15 points, 11 rebounds) in the rematch was close enough.

"If he's going to play like that, they might as well crown 'em now," said Johnson, presumably meaning the SEC Tournament and the Final Four next door in the Mercedes-Benz Superdome in three weeks. "Because it's going to take a really, really good basketball team on a good day to beat this group."

LSU (18-13) was a good team on a good day. Intent on making amends for the 74-50 loss to UK on Jan. 28, the Tigers met, if not exceeded, Johnson's back-to-basics request: Compete.

"Guys were pressuring us and we were thinking, 'What are you doing?'" said Anthony Davis, who contributed 12 points, 14 rebounds and six blocks. "We didn't come with the mind set to be strong with the ball."

Above: Terrence Jones was fouled by LSU's Johnny O'Bryant III in the first half of Kentucky's win. *Pablo Alcalá | Lexington Herald-Leader*

Right: Anthony Davis dunked in the second half as Kentucky beat LSU 60-51. *Pablo Alcalá | Lexington Herald-Leader*

SOUTHEASTERN
SEC
OURNAMENT
KENTUCKY
23
KENTUCKY
14

Terrence Jones was fouled by LSU's Johnny O'Bryant III (2) in the first half. *Pablo Alcalá | Lexington Herald-Leader*

Kentucky's 18 turnovers were its most since Jan. 3 (19 against Arkansas-Little Rock). UK players used words like "flat," "lackadaisical" and "sluggish" to describe the performance.

To describe LSU's play, UK Coach John Calipari used the word "desperate" as a compliment.

"They were playing out of desperation," he said. "And our players are so young, they didn't understand."

Jones' moment arrived when LSU matched its largest lead of the game, moving ahead 35-30 with 16:51 left. Giving the game a fleur-de-lis touch, Andre Stringer set the margin by stealing the ball from Marquis Teague and driving to a layup.

UK's 11th turnover enabled LSU to take a 12-2 advantage in points off turnovers. As UK called timeout, Johnson sensed Kentucky about to apply the coup de grace.

"I told them, 'Here comes the run,'" the LSU coach said. "And, again, it's hard for people to understand, but that's not a good team. That's a great team. They got great players. So they're going to make a push.

"And they made a push, and they did a good job of taking us out of some of our stuff, offensively. And, so be it."

Jones scored Kentucky's next nine points. He began the one-man 9-0 run by taking a patented Darius Miller lob from the lane and flushing it home.

Less than a minute later, Jones drove by Storm Warren for a dunk. That matchup proved telling as Kentucky (31-1) advanced to a Saturday semifinal game against Florida.

"They couldn't stop him off the dribble," Teague said of Jones. "We wanted to keep getting him the

Above: Michael Kidd-Gilchrist scored past LSU's Eddie Ludwig (13) in the first half. *Pablo Alcalá | Lexington Herald-Leader*

Below: Doron Lamb made a "3 goggles" sign after scoring in the first half against LSU. *Pablo Alcalá | Lexington Herald-Leader*

BOX SCORE

LSU

## Player Name	TOT-FG FG-FGA	3-PT FG-FGA	FT-FTA	REBOUNDS OF	DE	TOT	PF	TP	A	TO	BLK	S	MIN
24 WARREN, Storm....... f	6-15	0-0	2-2	3	3	6	3	14	0	1	1	1	29
41 HAMILTON, Justin.... c	1-12	0-1	2-4	1	6	7	1	4	1	1	3	0	33
01 HICKEY, Anthony..... g	5-13	0-4	0-0	1	2	3	2	10	4	1	0	5	40-
10 STRINGER, Andre..... g	4-15	1-4	2-2	1	2	3	2	11	2	2	0	4	38
22 TURNER, Ralston..... g	3-7	2-4	2-2	1	2	3	5	10	2	1	0	0	20
02 O'BRYANT III, Johnny	1-5	0-0	0-0	5	1	6	5	2	1	2	0	2	17
04 BASS, Chris.........	0-0	0-0	0-0	0	0	0	1	0	0	0	0	0	4
05 WHITE, Malcolm......	0-0	0-0	0-0	0	2	2	1	0	0	1	0	0	1
13 LUDWIG, Eddie.......	0-1	0-1	0-0	0	2	2	1	0	0	0	0	1	16
32 ISAAC, John.........	0-0	0-0	0-0	0	0	0	2	0	0	0	0	0	2
TEAM................				2	2	4							
Totals.............	20-68	3-14	8-10	14	22	36	23	51	10	9	4	13	200

TOTAL FG% 1st Half: 9-36 25.0% 2nd Half: 11-32 34.4% Game: 29.4% DEADB
3-Pt. FG% 1st Half: 2-10 20.0% 2nd Half: 1-4 25.0% Game: 21.4% REBS
F Throw % 1st Half: 4-6 66.7% 2nd Half: 4-4 100 % Game: 80.0% 1

KENTUCKY

## Player Name	TOT-FG FG-FGA	3-PT FG-FGA	FT-FTA	REBOUNDS OF	DE	TOT	PF	TP	A	TO	BLK	S	MIN
03 Jones, Terrence..... f	5-12	0-2	5-8	3	8	11	2	15	0	4	1	2	35
14 Kidd-Gilchrist, M... f	5-8	0-1	9-12	4	5	9	3	19	1	1	1	1	38
23 Davis, Anthony...... f	4-8	0-1	4-5	1	13	14	2	12	1	4	6	1	33
20 Lamb, Doron......... g	4-7	1-3	3-4	0	3	3	3	12	0	2	0	0	36
25 Teague, Marquis..... g	0-5	0-0	2-4	0	0	0	0	2	5	4	0	1	34
01 Miller, Darius......	0-2	0-1	0-0	1	1	2	3	0	1	3	0	0	17
33 Wiltjer, Kyle.......	0-0	0-0	0-0	0	0	0	1	0	0	0	1	0	7
TEAM...............					3	3							
Totals.............	18-42	1-8	23-33	9	33	42	14	60	8	18	9	5	200

TOTAL FG% 1st Half: 7-22 31.8% 2nd Half: 11-20 55.0% Game: 42.9% DEADB
3-Pt. FG% 1st Half: 1-4 25.0% 2nd Half: 0-4 0.0% Game: 12.5% REBS
F Throw % 1st Half: 10-16 62.5% 2nd Half: 13-17 76.5% Game: 69.7% 3,2

Officials: Antonio Petty, Mike Nance, Pat Adams

Technical fouls: LSU — None. Kentucky — None.

Attendance: 18,207

Score by Periods	1st	2nd	Total
LSU	24	27	51
Kentucky	25	35	60

ball until they found an answer to him."

Jones' put-back of a Miller miss put UK ahead for good at 37-35 with 14:18 left. His two free throws at the 12:10 mark widened the lead to four points.

Meanwhile, LSU missed seven straight shots in a scoreless five-minute span.

As a largely dressed-in-blue crowd cheered, Kentucky seemingly passed a baton from hero to hero.

With Davis in first-half foul trouble, Michael Kidd-Gilchrist became the go-to guy in the post.

Then Jones scored Kentucky to a lead.

Davis finished off LSU down the stretch.

But given what happened in Baton Rouge in late January, LSU's inability to keep up with Jones seemed most memorable.

"I love when he's playing that way," Kidd-Gilchrist said. "That's the 'T.J.' I know."

It's the "T.J." LSU knows all too well.■

WILDCATS 74
GATORS 71

NEW ORLEANS — MARCH 10, 2012

BY: JERRY TIPTON — SEC TOURNAMENT: GAME 2

KENTUCKY STOPS FLORIDA 74-71 TO REACH SEC FINALS

Besides winning the championship, Kentucky carried an auxiliary goal into the Southeastern Conference Tournament: Require any opponent impudent enough to consider beating the Cats to play 40 minutes of solid basketball to do it.

Florida came close Saturday but fell just shy of the needed seamless good play. Kentucky won 74-71.

"They played great for just about 40 minutes," said point guard Marquis Teague, whose two free throws with 14.2 seconds left clinched UK's 32nd victory in 33 games.

"Just about" included 11-for-22 shooting from Florida's live-or-die three-point range. But for only the third time in 21 games this season, the Gators lost while making 10 or more three-point shots.

"We took a really good shot from them and LSU," Terrence Jones said of UK's two victories in two days. "We really stepped up to the challenge."

Kentucky used a big second-half rebounding effort to beat Florida and advance to the SEC Tournament's championship game Sunday. During a decisive 14-0 run that erased Florida's 56-51 lead, the Cats grabbed six offensive rebounds.

After assuming a 65-56 lead entering the final seven minutes, Kentucky appeared to be on cruise control.

"I believe, this time, we didn't give up," Florida freshman Bradley Beal said. "In the first two games (against UK), we kind of gave up down the stretch."

Florida (23-10) closed within two, 65-63. Then Anthony Davis outfought two Florida players for a

Terrence Jones dunked over Florida's Cody Larson in the first half of the semifinal game of the SEC tournament in New Orleans. *Pablo Alcalá | Lexington Herald-Leader*

Michael Kidd-Gilchrist puts up a shot against Florida's Erik Murphy (33) in the second half of their SEC tournament game. *Pablo Alcalá | Lexington Herald-Leader*

rebound of Teague's missed free throw. The put-back put the Cats ahead 68-63 going into the final two minutes.

Kentucky led once in the first half: A Davis three-pointer with 13.1 seconds left put the Cats up 40-39.

For much of the first half, UK lived its worst nightmare against Florida. The Gators made three-pointers (five of its first eight attempts) and got good work from Patric Young in the low post against Davis. While the three-point accuracy departed from the track record (Florida made only 12 of 49 attempts in the two regular-season games), Young proved productive against Davis for the second time in seven days.

A three-pointer by Beal with 8:42 left gave Florida its largest lead: 31-21. That marked only the second game all season that Kentucky trailed by a double-digit margin, the first time coming at Mississippi State on Feb. 21.

Unlike at Starkville, Kentucky did not wait until the second half to rally. The Cats held Florida scoreless over the final 4:24 of the first half. In that span, the Gators missed seven shots (two from beyond the arc), and UK steadily closed.

Teague used a hesitation dribble to freeze Erving Walker before hitting a pull-up jumper to bring Kentucky within two, 39-37. After Kenny Boynton missed an ill-advised driving shot over Davis, the UK freshman star hit a three-pointer from the left wing.

The shot marked the third straight game Davis had made a three-pointer.

Florida did not go away early in the second half. Three-pointers by Erik Murphy and Beal — which

Terrence Jones drove past Florida's Bradley Beal in the second half. *Pablo Alcalá | Lexington Herald-Leader*

made the Gators 7-for-13 from beyond the arc till then — helped put Kentucky behind 49-47 at the first TV timeout of the second half.

Beal's three-pointer with 17:53 left was Florida's seventh, or one more than the Gators had in either of their regular-season games against Kentucky.

Kentucky fan frustration — or impatience — began to show midway through the second half. A five-shot possession that yielded no points? There had to be a foul in there somewhere, the booing suggested.

Later, Young used his considerable muscle to clear space for a rebound. Again, no foul and plenty of boos.

Florida took a 54-49 lead when Walker hit a three-pointer with 11:40 left. It was his first basket (after six misses). Until that shot, he'd made only 23 of 95 (15 of 54 from beyond the arc) against UK in his career.

Kentucky regained the lead with a five-point flurry in less than a minute. After two Jones free throws, Michael Kidd-Gilchrist hit a floater. Then

BOX SCORE

FLORIDA

## Player Name	TOT-FG FG-FGA	3-PT FG-FGA	FT-FTA	REBOUNDS OF	DE	TOT	PF	TP	A	TO	BLK	S	MIN
33 Murphy, Erik........ f	9-12	4-4	2-2	1	2	3	4	24	0	1	0	0	32
04 Young, Patric....... c	5-9	0-0	0-0	3	2	5	2	10	1	1	0	0	27
01 Boynton, Kenny...... g	1-9	0-4	0-0	0	1	1	2	2	4	1	0	0	33
11 Walker, Erving...... g	3-10	2-5	0-0	0	1	1	1	8	4	1	0	1	34
23 Beal, Bradley....... g	8-15	4-7	0-0	2	6	8	2	20	5	0	1	1	37
03 Rosario, Mike.......	0-0	0-0	0-0	0	0	0	0	0	0	1	0	0	2
05 Wilbekin, Scottie...	2-3	1-2	0-0	0	2	2	2	5	4	1	0	1	19
24 Prather, Casey......	1-2	0-0	0-0	0	1	1	2	2	0	2	0	0	8
34 Larson, Cody........	0-0	0-0	0-0	0	1	1	0	0	0	0	0	0	8
TEAM...............				1	2	3							
Totals.............	29-60	11-22	2-2	7	18	25	15	71	18	8	1	3	200

TOTAL FG%	1st Half:	16-33 48.5%	2nd Half:	13-27 48.1%	Game: 48.3%	DEADB
3-Pt. FG%	1st Half:	5-11 45.5%	2nd Half:	6-11 54.5%	Game: 50.0%	REBS
F Throw %	1st Half:	2-2 100 %	2nd Half:	0-0 0.0%	Game: 100 %	1,1

KENTUCKY

## Player Name	TOT-FG FG-FGA	3-PT FG-FGA	FT-FTA	REBOUNDS OF	DE	TOT	PF	TP	A	TO	BLK	S	MIN
03 Jones, Terrence..... f	5-13	1-3	4-4	4	5	9	1	15	1	1	0	1	33
14 Kidd-Gilchrist, M... f	3-5	0-1	4-6	5	3	8	2	10	1	1	1	1	39
23 Davis, Anthony...... f	6-13	1-2	2-4	5	7	12	1	15	3	0	2	1	37
20 Lamb, Doron......... g	6-14	2-5	2-2	0	2	2	1	16	0	0	0	0	36
25 Teague, Marquis..... g	6-9	0-1	3-4	1	2	3	1	15	5	3	0	1	35
01 Miller, Darius......	0-3	0-2	0-0	0	1	1	2	0	3	1	1	1	13
33 Wiltjer, Kyle.......	1-3	1-3	0-0	0	1	1	0	3	1	0	0	0	7
TEAM...............				1	2	3							
Totals.............	27-60	5-17	15-20	16	23	39	8	74	14	6	4	5	200

TOTAL FG%	1st Half:	18-31 58.1%	2nd Half:	9-29 31.0%	Game: 45.0%	DEADB
3-Pt. FG%	1st Half:	3-9 33.3%	2nd Half:	2-8 25.0%	Game: 29.4%	REBS
F Throw %	1st Half:	1-2 50.0%	2nd Half:	14-18 77.8%	Game: 75.0%	3

Officials: Anthony Jordan, Gary Maxwell, Ron Groover

Technical fouls: Florida — None. Kentucky — None.

Attendance: 18,523

Score by Periods	1st	2nd	Total
Florida	39	32	71
Kentucky	40	34	74

Doron Lamb took a shot over Florida's Casey Prather in the first half. *Pablo Alcalá | Lexington Herald-Leader*

Doron Lamb separated Scottie Wilbekin from the ball and sped to a layup that put the Cats ahead 57-56.

A Florida timeout interrupted, but failed to halt, Kentucky's momentum. Jones hit a three-pointer, then dunked a missed flip shot by Davis to put UK ahead 62-56 with less than eight minutes left.

The lead grew as large as 65-56 going into the final seven minutes.

"I think we're starting to figure out we're a team that, outside of Patric, when he's off the floor, we really don't necessarily have a dominant post presence," Florida Coach Billy Donovan said. "Kentucky's got three of them."

Donovan meant Kidd-Gilchrist, Jones and Davis.

"And even (Darius) Miller," the Florida coach said.

Even on one of Florida's better days, that was too much to overcome.■

VS. VANDERBILT

COMMODORES 71
WILDCATS 64

NEW ORLEANS MARCH 11, 2012

BY: JOHN CLAY SEC TOURNAMENT: GAME 3

LOSS BRINGS MANY QUESTIONS

Most important: Was it a good thing?

So now we will see if the theory is true.

The theory being that you don't want to go into the NCAA Tournament carrying a long winning streak, that the pressure is too great, the load too heavy.

Conventional wisdom says that these days when competitive parity is king, better to lose a game before you get to the Big Dance than to have your heart broken in the Big Dance.

And yet, when March arrives, win or lose, surely a team wants to be playing its best basketball of the season.

The fact of the matter is that Kentucky's 71-64 loss to a good Vanderbilt team in the finals of the SEC Tournament at the New Orleans Arena was not exactly an anomaly.

Kentucky did not play particularly well in any of the three games here.

It struggled for most of the game with a middling LSU team that was on the NIT bubble before finally putting away Trent Johnson's Tigers 60-51 on Friday.

Back in January, the Cats had beaten LSU by 24 in Baton Rouge.

In Saturday's semifinal, UK held off Florida 74-71.

That's the same Florida the Cats beat by 20 points in Lexington, and by 15 points just last Sunday in Gainesville.

Plus, on Saturday, the Gators shot the best percentage (48.3) against a Kentucky defense since eventual national champ Connecticut shot 57.7 percent in whipping the Cats in the Maui

Terrence Jones defended against Vanderbilt's Festus Ezeli in the second half. *Pablo Alcalá | Lexington Herald-Leader*

Invitational finals last season.

Then Sunday, before a crowd of 18,114, in which 18,104 appeared to be Kentucky fans, the Cats failed to score a field goal in the final 8:03 and were outscored 16-2 over the final five minutes.

The Cats missed their last 13 shots.

"We lost at the end of the game," admitted Terrence Jones. "But we didn't make plays the first half."

"We should have been up 10 at halftime," said Coach John Calipari, before later remarking about the loss, "I wish this would have happened yesterday so we got home a day earlier, but ..."

Maybe UK's play had something to do with the head coach's mind-set. He made no bones about his dislike for the post-season affair, all but saying he wished his team could blow off the trip to New Orleans.

In the first two games, Kentucky got little to nothing from its two top reserves, Darius Miller and Kyle Wiltjer, who scored a grand total of three points.

Sunday, Kentucky made six of 28 three-pointers for 21.4 percent. The last time UK shot that many threes and shot that low a percentage was the 2010 NCAA Tournament loss to West Virginia. You remember that one. UK was eliminated after making just four of 32 threes for 12.5 percent.

Overall, the Cats shot 35.9 percent, their lowest shooting percentage since shooting 29.8 percent in that ugly win over Louisville on New Year's Eve.

Now the question: Was this just an aberration?

Vanderbilt s Rod Odom blocked a shot by Doron Lamb in the second half.
Pablo Alcalá | Lexington Herald-Leader

Did a young Kentucky team, without a deep bench, succumb to the fatigue of playing three games in three days? Did the law of averages catch up with the Cats?

Or how about giving Vanderbilt credit. In the two previous meetings, Vanderbilt was right there at the end.

They led UK 63-61 with 4:08 left in Nashville, but couldn't hold on. They trailed UK 66-65 with 4:22 left in Lexington, but couldn't hang with the home team the rest of the way.

This time, Vanderbilt was the team that made the final push.

Does it simply mean that for Vanderbilt, the third time was the charm?

"It's hard to beat a good team three times," said UK center Anthony Davis. "And Vandy is a good team."

Or, for some reason, has Kentucky lost the edge it had during that 24-game win streak?

"We've just got to get back in the gym," Davis said. "Get refocused."

And will Sunday's loss allow the Cats to reclaim that edge?

We are about to find out.■

Anthony Davis shot over Vanderbilt's Steve Tchiengang in the second half of the SEC tournament championship game. *Pablo Alcalá | Lexington Herald-Leader*

Above: Darius Miller and Anthony Davis were down on the floor as Vanderbilt's Jeffery Taylor left with the ball in the second half. Vanderbilt upset Kentucky 71-64 to capture the SEC tournament championship. *Pablo Alcalá | Lexington Herald-Leader*

Below: Darius Miller walked off the court after UK lost the SEC tournament championship game. *Pablo Alcalá | Lexington Herald-Leader*

BOX SCORE

VANDERBILT

## Player Name	TOT-FG FG-FGA	3-PT FG-FGA	FT-FTA	REBOUNDS OF	DE	TOT	PF	TP	A	TO	BLK	S	MIN
05 GOULBOURNE, Lance... f	3-5	0-0	0-2	2	3	5	3	6	0	0	0	1	31
44 Taylor, Jeffery..... f	6-13	2-4	4-8	1	10	11	2	18	0	1	0	2	34
03 Ezeli, Festus....... c	5-9	0-0	7-10	4	2	6	5	17	0	2	1	0	32
01 Tinsley, Brad....... g	2-6	1-3	0-0	0	1	1	2	5	4	3	0	0	20
23 Jenkins, John....... g	3-12	3-10	8-9	0	7	7	0	17	2	3	1	0	36
02 Johnson, Kedren.....	2-4	0-1	2-3	0	1	1	1	6	2	1	0	0	23
24 Parker, Dai-Jon.....	0-1	0-0	0-0	0	0	0	0	0	0	0	0	1	7
33 Tchiengang, Steve...	1-1	0-0	0-0	2	3	5	1	2	0	1	0	1	10
45 Odom, Rod...........	0-0	0-0	0-0	0	0	0	2	0	0	0	0	0	7
TEAM................				3	1	4	1						
Totals..............	22-51	6-18	21-32	12	28	40	17	71	8	11	2	5	200

TOTAL FG%	1st Half:	13-27 48.1%	2nd Half:	9-24 37.5%	Game:	43.1%	DEADB
3-Pt. FG%	1st Half:	5-9 55.6%	2nd Half:	1-9 11.1%	Game:	33.3%	REBS
F Throw %	1st Half:	6-9 66.7%	2nd Half:	15-23 65.2%	Game:	65.6%	5,2

KENTUCKY

## Player Name	TOT-FG FG-FGA	3-PT FG-FGA	FT-FTA	REBOUNDS OF	DE	TOT	PF	TP	A	TO	BLK	S	MIN
03 Jones, Terrence..... f	5-11	1-3	1-3	4	7	11	3	12	0	2	1	2	33
23 Davis, Anthony...... f	4-9	0-3	4-8	4	6	10	3	12	2	0	3	1	34
01 Miller, Darius...... g	7-17	2-9	0-0	1	2	3	1	16	4	1	1	2	35
20 Lamb, Doron......... g	2-11	1-7	6-6	1	0	1	4	11	0	2	0	0	32
25 Teague, Marquis..... g	0-7	0-2	0-0	1	2	3	3	0	6	0	0	1	37
10 Beckham, Twany......	0-0	0-0	0-0	0	0	0	0	0	0	0	0	0	0+
14 Kidd-Gilchrist, M...	2-4	0-1	1-2	0	0	0	5	5	0	2	0	0	16
30 Vargas, Eloy........	0-1	0-0	0-0	1	0	1	1	0	0	0	0	0	2
33 Wiltjer, Kyle.......	3-4	2-3	0-0	0	1	1	2	8	0	1	3	0	11
TEAM................				3	4	7							
Totals..............	23-64	6-28	12-19	15	22	37	22	64	12	8	8	6	200

TOTAL FG%	1st Half:	14-35 40.0%	2nd Half:	9-29 31.0%	Game:	35.9%	DEADB
3-Pt. FG%	1st Half:	4-16 25.0%	2nd Half:	2-12 16.7%	Game:	21.4%	REBS
F Throw %	1st Half:	5-7 71.4%	2nd Half:	7-12 58.3%	Game:	63.2%	3,1

Officials: Tony Greene, Antinio Petty, Mike Nance

Technical fouls: Vanderbilt — TEAM. Kentucky — None.

Attendance: 18,114

Score by Periods	1st	2nd	Total
Vanderbilt	37	34	71
Kentucky	37	27	64

#25 MARQUIS TEAGUE

BY: JOHN CLAY　　WILDCAT FEATURE

LISTENING AND LEARNING

UK's Teague shows he's getting the point

Marquis Teague had no idea what people were saying about him.

"Only reason I found out was because Coach Cal told me," he said Saturday.

Coach Cal being John Calipari, of course, the man who broke the awful, terrible news to Kentucky's freshman point guard.

Halfway through Teague's rookie season, the caustic critics with their itchy trigger fingers were already labeling last year's No. 1 prep point guard as a collegiate disappointment.

Not that Calipari agreed, mind you.

"He's playing in Kentucky, for the second-ranked team in the country, that probably could easily be undefeated, and everybody's saying he's a disappointment," said the coach on Saturday just after his Cats opened SEC play by swatting away visiting South Carolina 79-64.

"What are you talking about? The kid is doing fine."

But, then:

"Now I expect more out of him," said Calipari, "but you shouldn't."

Laughter.

"I'm coaching him."

We're just the ones watching Teague, and analyzing Teague, and comparing Teague to his star-studded predecessors, like Brandon Knight, and John Wall, and even Tyreke Evans (Calipari point guard star at Memphis) and Derrick Rose (the Calipari point guard star at Memphis who got this point guard roll of all rolls started).

So far, anyway, Teague hadn't quite measured up to those ridiculously unrealistic measurements.

His perimeter shooting has been off target. He turned it over too much. He sometimes appeared to be more concerned with his own point total than his more altruistic responsibilities as a point guard. He was playing like, well, a freshman.

The problem is we are not used to John Calipari's freshman point guards playing like freshmen.

Ah, but Saturday, in the Cats' SEC opener, the Indianapolis native took one giant step toward being the point guard both Calipari and the fans want.

Marquis Teague shot a jumper over Iowa State's Bubu Palo in the NCAA tournament in Louisville.
Charles Bertram | Lexington Herald-Leader

He scored a career-high 17 points, hitting six of 10 shots, including his only three-point attempt. He was four-of-five from the free throw line. He had four assists, two turnovers one steal.

The point guard was on point.

"Yeah," said a smiling Teague afterward. "This probably was my best overall game so far."

What made it so?

"I was just slowing it down more," he said, "looking to get my teammates involved more."

Not that Teague has played badly, mind you.

"Here he is, he's a freshman," said Calipari. "He's played in 16 college games, 15 before this game. Because he wasn't playing perfect — he had 4.5 assists and three turnovers. That ain't bad. And if he passed it a couple of more times, he'd be averaging six assists and three turnovers which is perfect."

But for this team to get where it and its fans want to go, the Cats need a point guard who is better than "ain't bad."

This team doesn't need a Brandon Knight, who carried so much of last year's scoring load. It doesn't need a John Wall, whose outrageous talent comes along only so often.

It needs a point guard who complements his teammates, who takes the points when they come, and does what his coach wants.

"He's started listening," said UK center Anthony Davis. "And when he starts listening, great things start to happen. He was listening during the press attack, bringing the ball up, to what Coach Cal wanted him to do. He's starting to listen and he's starting to get open shots."

Indeed, Calipari had said that if Teague does the other things he is supposed to do, the scoring thing will work out, too.

"Yeah," said Teague, "I was just trying to do whatever he told me to do, run the team and not turn the ball over and it was successful for me."

That Marquis Teague meets expectations every time.■

Marquis Teague reacted to a Terrence Jones dunk against Morehouse College in Rupp Arena. *Charles Bertram | Lexington Herald-Leader*

VS. WESTERN KENTUCKY

WILDCATS 81
HILLTOPPERS 66

KFC YUM! CENTER **MARCH 15, 2012**

BY: JERRY TIPTON

NCAA TOURNAMENT: GAME 1

1 DOWN, 5 TO GO

Cats dominate Hilltoppers in all phases, dazzle in opener

A telling moment in Kentucky's 81-66 victory over Western Kentucky on Thursday night came early in the second half. That's when UK Coach John Calipari instructed Anthony Davis on dunking etiquette after the freshman received a technical foul for hanging onto the rim a tad too long.

With dunks accounting for six of its first 12 second-half baskets, UK got plenty of practice in perfecting basketball's ultimate take-that.

A thumping of Western in the NCAA Tournament's second round served multiple purposes. It improved UK's record to 33-2, faded the memory of Sunday's loss to Vanderbilt in the Southeastern Conference Tournament finals and propelled the Cats to a game Saturday against Iowa State, a 77-64 winner over Connecticut later Thursday night.

Maybe most important, Kentucky met its goal of re-establishing a running game, which led to the many dunks.

The Cats reminded everyone of "our identity being a transition team," said Terrence Jones, whose 22 points and 10 rebounds marked his third double-double in the last five games.

"We felt teams were thinking we were out of shape," Jones said. Florida center Patric Young said just that in the SEC Tournament.

"We weren't tired," Jones said. "That was crazy. We're one of the most in-shape teams in the country."

Western, which came into the game with a Ratings Percentage Index of No. 189, finished the season at 16-19. The Hilltoppers were the 21st team to play in the NCAA Tournament despite a losing regular-season record.

Above: Terrence Jones dunked over WKU's Teeng Akol in the second half. *Charles Bertram | Lexington Herald-Leader*

Right: Darius Miller dunked for two of his 6 points as top-seeded Kentucky defeated Western Kentucky University. *Mark Cornelison | Lexington Herald-Leader*

NCAA
KENTUCKY
1
KENTUCKY
3
WKU
WKU
41
WKU
14
EAST REGION
MIDWEST REGION

Marquis Teague scored on a drive to the basket as UK beat Western Kentucky University in the KFC Yum Center in Louisville. *Charles Bertram | Lexington Herald-Leader*

Before a Western shot hit the rim, Kentucky led 6-0.

Although the Hilltoppers competed well, Kentucky cruised to a 45-26 halftime lead. That marked UK's largest halftime lead since a 27-point bulge at South Carolina on Feb. 4.

Jones and Doron Lamb, relative graybeards as sophomores, led the offense. Jones scored 15 first-half points, which represented more than he'd had in 19 previous games this season.

Lamb added 14 (or more than he'd had in 18 previous games). Each player made six of eight shots to lead Kentucky's blistering 61.5 percent shooting half.

"I know I was a little nervous (as a freshman)," Jones said in welcoming a leadership role. "And the pressure last year (on freshmen) wasn't like this year."

Jones and Lamb accounted for nine of UK's first 10 points. The Cats led 10-0 less than three minutes into the game.

While UK went to Jones in the post on its first possession, Western tried to answer with George Fant. But Fant hit only the backboard on his shot.

With T.J. Price hitting a pair of three-pointers, Western took a 12-10 lead.

But the Hilltoppers' only lead of the game vanished within 28 seconds. Jones put UK ahead for good at 14-12 on a layup with 13:58 left. The shot gave Jones 1,001 points in his two-season UK career. He finished at 1,017.

As the second half began, Kentucky quickly dashed any Western hopes of mounting one of its signature comebacks. The Hilltoppers rallied from 16 down in the final five minutes in the First Four victory Tuesday over Mississippi Valley State.

On its first possession of the second half Thursday, guard Jamal Crook threw a low-post feed too far in front of Fant. The ball went out of bounds, and WKU Coach Ray Harper sat back in his seat and threw up his hands.

Jones put an exclamation on a big night for himself and Kentucky by taking a fast-break pass from Marquis Teague and soaring to a one-handed dunk over 6-foot-11 Teeng Akol.

"He's the same guy," teammate Darius Miller said of Jones' big night. "He's just taking it upon himself to dominate the game."

With Jones leading the way, Kentucky got what Miller called the "easy baskets in transition" that blew away Western.

One caveat: UK got to run despite only forcing 10

Doron Lamb scored over WKU's Kene Anyigbo in the first half. *Charles Bertram | Lexington Herald-Leader*

BOX SCORE

WESTERN KENTUCKY

## Player Name	TOT-FG FG-FGA	3-PT FG-FGA	FT-FTA	REBOUNDS OF	DE	TOT	PF	TP	A	TO	BLK	S	MIN
44 Fant, George........ f	6-14	0-0	1-1	1	3	4	2	13	0	1	0	3	32
22 Akol, Teeng......... c	1-7	0-1	0-0	0	3	3	1	2	1	1	1	0	22
05 Gordon, Derrick..... g	6-11	0-1	0-0	0	5	5	1	12	0	0	0	0	36
14 Crook, Jamal........ g	1-6	0-0	1-2	1	2	3	2	3	2	2	0	1	17
52 Price, T.J.......... g	6-11	3-7	6-7	1	3	4	5	21	0	0	0	0	33
00 Anyigbo, Kene.......	1-1	0-0	0-0	0	0	0	1	2	0	2	0	0	3
03 McDonald, Kahlil....	4-11	3-6	2-4	0	3	3	2	13	5	1	1	1	31
11 Sheldon, Spence.....	0-0	0-0	0-0	0	0	0	0	0	0	0	0	0	0+
15 Akamune, O'Karo.....	0-1	0-0	0-2	2	0	2	1	0	0	0	0	0	9
21 Snipes, Nigel.......	0-0	0-0	0-0	1	0	1	0	0	0	1	0	1	4
41 Zollo, Vinny........	0-1	0-0	0-0	1	1	2	4	0	2	2	0	0	13
TEAM................				3		3							
Totals..............	25-63	6-15	10-16	10	20	30	19	66	10	10	2	6	200

TOTAL FG%	1st Half:	10-32 31.3%	2nd Half:	15-31 48.4%	Game:	39.7%	DEADB
3-Pt. FG%	1st Half:	2-7 28.6%	2nd Half:	4-8 50.0%	Game:	40.0%	REBS
F Throw %	1st Half:	4-7 57.1%	2nd Half:	6-9 66.7%	Game:	62.5%	3

KENTUCKY

## Player Name	TOT-FG FG-FGA	3-PT FG-FGA	FT-FTA	REBOUNDS OF	DE	TOT	PF	TP	A	TO	BLK	S	MIN
03 Jones, Terrence..... f	9-13	1-2	3-3	2	8	10	2	22	2	1	0	1	35
14 Kidd-Gilchrist, M... f	4-8	0-1	1-3	1	6	7	3	9	2	2	1	0	34
23 Davis, Anthony...... f	5-8	0-0	6-8	2	7	9	0	16	3	0	7	1	36
20 Lamb, Doron......... g	7-12	2-4	0-0	1	3	4	2	16	0	3	0	0	29
25 Teague, Marquis..... g	3-7	0-1	6-8	0	2	2	1	12	4	3	0	0	32
01 Miller, Darius......	2-4	0-0	2-3	1	3	4	3	6	3	0	0	0	26
05 Polson, Jarrod......	0-0	0-0	0-0	0	0	0	0	0	0	0	0	0	0+
10 Beckham, Twany......	0-0	0-0	0-0	0	0	0	0	0	0	0	0	0	0+
30 Vargas, Eloy........	0-0	0-0	0-0	1	0	1	0	0	0	0	0	0	0+
32 Long, Brian.........	0-0	0-0	0-0	0	0	0	0	0	0	0	0	0	0+
33 Wiltjer, Kyle.......	0-2	0-2	0-0	1	1	2	3	0	0	3	1	0	8
TEAM................													
Totals..............	30-54	3-10	18-25	9	30	39	14	81	14	12	9	2	200

TOTAL FG%	1st Half:	16-26 61.5%	2nd Half:	14-28 50.0%	Game:	55.6%	DEADB
3-Pt. FG%	1st Half:	2-5 40.0%	2nd Half:	1-5 20.0%	Game:	30.0%	REBS
F Throw %	1st Half:	11-13 84.6%	2nd Half:	7-12 58.3%	Game:	72.0%	2,1

Officials: Gerry Pollard, Edwin Edsall, Jerry Heater

Technical fouls: Western Kentucky — None. Kentucky — Davis, Anthony.

Attendance: 22,131

Score by Periods	1st	2nd	Total
Western Kentucky	26	40	66
Kentucky	45	36	81

Western turnovers. Good defense (the Hilltoppers made only 10 of their first 37 shots) ignited the UK break.

"We want to make teams keep up with us," Miller said.

Western didn't score until almost three minutes into the second half.

By then, Kentucky led 50-26 and bore no resemblance to Mississippi Valley State.

The technical on Davis came with 14:22 left. He also got one at Mississippi State on Feb. 21.

"They said I pulled myself up," Davis said of the latest technical foul. "I thought I was going to fall. The refs saw it otherwise."

As Western got ready to shoot the technical free throws, Calipari called over Davis and raised both hands in a grasping motion.

Calipari told Davis the player's safety comes first.

"He said just hang on the rim," Davis said.■

VS. IOWA STATE

WILDCATS 87
CYCLONES 71

KFC YUM! CENTER — MARCH 17, 2012

BY: JERRY TIPTON — NCAA TOURNAMENT: GAME 2

CATS TAKE IT OUTSIDE

Cyclones own paint but Cats triumph at arc

Iowa State mostly kept Kentucky away from the basket. But Kentucky put the ball in the basket often enough to win 87-71 Saturday to advance to the NCAA Tournament's Sweet 16.

Marquis Teague's career-high 24 points and Darius Miller's season-high 19 points enabled UK to breeze without its customary scoring dominance in the paint.

Kentucky (34-2) didn't come close to its average of 36.7 "paint points" coming into the NCAA Tournament. UK barely got half the 46 points from the paint it posted - no pun intended - in smothering Western Kentucky here Thursday.

Iowa State limited UK to 24 points from the lane, which equaled its second-lowest total of the season.

So what?

"Everybody, they want to talk about our three-point shooting," UK Coach John Calipari said. "We're one of the best in the country. We just don't shoot a lot."

UK, which ranked No. 58 in the country in three-point accuracy (37 percent), had made 10 or more three-pointers only four times all season before 10-of-20 accuracy foiled Iowa State's customary collapse-into-the-lane defense.

Noting UK's 15-for-63 three-point shooting in the four most recent games, Iowa State Coach Fred Hoiberg gambled that the misfires would continue.

"You have to take something away from them," he said.

Iowa State (23-11) outscored UK in the paint but made only two of their first 18 three-point shots. Iowa State made a season-low three three-pointers. That wasn't nearly enough support for star Royce

Above: Darius Miller signaled a three pointer as top-seeded Kentucky played Iowa State. *Mark Cornelison | Lexington Herald-Leader*

Right: Anthony Davis blocked the shot of Iowa State forward Royce White. *Mark Cornelison | Lexington Herald-Leader*

NCAA
Wilson
DAVIS
23
3

White, who led Iowa State with 23 points and nine rebounds.

"Our biggest strength is the three-point shot, and we go three-for-22," Hoiberg said. "We're not going to win very many games when we shoot the ball like that."

If Iowa State, which suffered its most lopsided loss of the season, intended to keep Kentucky away from the basket, the strategy worked in the first half.

But UK rode perimeter shooting to a 38-27 halftime lead. The Cats took the initiative by making 10 of their first 18 shots to take control. Three-pointers by Kyle Wiltjer and Miller were part of a 10-0 run that gave UK its largest first-half lead at 23-11.

"I told our guys, 'Look, Darius, you and Doron (Lamb) must shoot the ball because they're going to give those to you,'" Calipari said. "'If they rush you, drive them into the middle of the lane. They're not going to leave Anthony Davis. You'll get something.'"

Teague, whose 13 first-half points included his first three-pointer since the regular-season finale at Florida, gave Kentucky its

Marquis Teague went in for two of his career-high 24 points against Iowa State.
Mark Cornelison | Lexington Herald-Leader

largest lead with a fast-break layup.

"I didn't really care about scoring points, really," Teague said. "I just wanted to get my teammates involved."

White scored easy as you please on the game's first possession and seemed headed for a big night. He posted up against Terrence Jones and went around him for a layup on the game's first possession.

White scored nine of Iowa State's first 11 points, then went silent. He took only one shot in the half's final 14 minutes.

"We were just watching his eyes," Davis said. "If he was looking up, he was looking to pass. And if he's (looking) down, he just wants to score the ball."

The Cyclones' only three of the first half — by Melvin Ejim, a 20.8-percent shooter from beyond the arc — reduced UK's lead to 26-22 with seven minutes left.

Kentucky held Iowa State to one basket the rest of the half. A 21-11 rebounding advantage helped keep the Cats comfortably ahead.

But Kentucky's lead vanished before the first TV time-out of the second half.

White led the charge. Twice he drove for easy scores, on the second he ripped the ball from a posting Davis and drove the length of the court for a dunk over Jones. That play reduced UK's lead to 38-34.

Iowa State tied on a heady driving layup in which Scott Christopherson used the rim to screen Davis.

Dunks by Jones and Davis pushed Kentucky ahead 48-42, prompting an Iowa State time-out.

A phantom foul on Lamb — his fourth — caused UK fan anxiety. But Kentucky countered without its best perimeter shooter.

A fast-break Miller three-pointer made it 53-44, prompting another Iowa State time-out.

But after the Cyclones missed two more three-pointers, Teague took a pass from Davis and scored while being fouled. The basket gave him a career-high 17 points.

The lead grew to as much as 76-52 on a Teague layup.

During the post-game handshake, Calipari told Hoiberg that Iowa State caught Kentucky on one of its better days.

"I said that's about as good as we can play," Calipari said. "We played good. I've got a good basketball team. You won't believe this (but) I've got good players, too. But they're a good team."■

BOX SCORE

IOWA STATE

	TOT-FG	3-PT		REBOUNDS									
## Player Name	FG-FGA	FG-FGA	FT-FTA	OF	DE	TOT	PF	TP	A	TO	BLK	S	MIN
03 Ejim, Melvin........ f	1-5	1-2	1-4	6	3	9	1	4	0	0	1	1	30
30 White, Royce........ f	9-12	0-0	5-9	1	8	9	5	23	4	3	1	3	34
02 Babb, Chris......... g	0-2	0-2	0-0	0	4	4	2	0	0	0	0	0	27
04 Allen, Chris........ g	6-19	1-10	3-3	1	0	1	1	16	0	0	0	0	37
11 Christopherson,Scott g	5-11	1-4	4-4	0	2	2	0	15	3	1	0	0	31
01 Palo, Bubu..........	1-2	0-0	2-2	0	1	1	5	4	0	0	0	1	11
22 Booker, Anthony.....	0-3	0-1	0-0	3	1	4	1	0	0	1	0	0	6
24 Gibson, Percy.......	3-4	0-0	3-3	0	0	0	1	9	0	1	0	0	10
25 McGee, Tyrus........	0-3	0-3	0-0	1	0	1	1	0	0	1	0	1	14
TEAM................							1						
Totals.............	25-61	3-22	18-25	12	19	31	18	71	7	7	2	6	200

TOTAL FG%	1st Half:	10-26 38.5%	2nd Half:	15-35 42.9%	Game:	41.0%	DEADB
3-Pt. FG%	1st Half:	1-8 12.5%	2nd Half:	2-14 14.3%	Game:	13.6%	REBS
F Throw %	1st Half:	6-7 85.7%	2nd Half:	12-18 66.7%	Game:	72.0%	3

KENTUCKY

	TOT-FG	3-PT		REBOUNDS									
## Player Name	FG-FGA	FG-FGA	FT-FTA	OF	DE	TOT	PF	TP	A	TO	BLK	S	MIN
03 Jones, Terrence..... f	3-9	0-1	2-4	4	7	11	5	8	3	1	2	1	33
14 Kidd-Gilchrist, M... f	1-4	0-1	0-0	2	5	7	2	2	1	2	0	0	33
23 Davis, Anthony...... f	4-9	0-1	7-9	4	8	12	2	15	5	3	2	0	40-
20 Lamb, Doron......... g	5-8	5-7	1-2	0	0	0	4	16	0	1	0	0	20
25 Teague, Marquis... g	10-14	1-3	3-5	1	3	4	2	24	7	2	0	1	36
01 Miller, Darius......	7-11	3-6	2-2	1	5	6	3	19	3	1	1	0	35
33 Wiltjer, Kyle.......	1-1	1-1	0-0	0	0	0	1	3	0	0	0	0	3
TEAM................										1			
Totals.............	31-56	10-20	15-22	12	28	40	19	87	19	11	5	2	200

TOTAL FG%	1st Half:	15-31 48.4%	2nd Half:	16-25 64.0%	Game:	55.4%	DEADB
3-Pt. FG%	1st Half:	4-13 30.8%	2nd Half:	6-7 85.7%	Game:	50.0%	REBS
F Throw %	1st Half:	4-4 100 %	2nd Half:	11-18 61.1%	Game:	68.2%	1

Officials: Jamie Luckie, Sean Corbin, Gerry Pollard

Technical fouls: Iowa State — TEAM. Kentucky — Jones, Terrence.

Attendance: 21,757

Score by Periods	1st	2nd	Total
Iowa State	27	44	71
Kentucky	38	49	87

Michael Kidd-Gilchrist let out a yell after a UK run forced an Iowa State time out. *Mark Cornelison | Lexington Herald-Leader*

COACH JOHN CALIPARI

BY: JOHN CLAY

WILDCAT FEATURE

TITLE IS ALL THAT REMAINS FOR CALIPARI

Coach has achieved fans' other goals

There is really only one thing left. John Calipari has done it all since he came to Kentucky three seasons ago.

Well, almost.

He's put Kentucky back in the win column. Remember that before Billy Gillispie was forced out the door after his two-year reign of terror, which followed Tubby Smith's slide into mediocrity, UK basketball was a once-premier program that had not reached the measuring stick of the Final Four since 1998.

The Cats weren't great. They were once great.

Calipari has assembled the best talent. Near the end of his 10-year term, Smith was known for his just-misses on the recruiting trail. He kept taking those disappointing phone calls from recruits who decided to go elsewhere. Gillispie got commitments from eighth-graders.

Calipari gets commitments from players who in reality are pros, but because of ridiculous rules, must play one year in college. They want to spend that one year with Calipari. The reason is that Calipari assures they will end up in the pros.

It's the reason why under Calipari, Kentucky has had the No. 1 recruiting class three years running.

He's put Kentucky back in the forefront. To be honest, UK basketball fans have always been a little over the top. Calipari is right there with them and beyond. He's talking Kentucky Effect and "we are the needle" and feeding the beast that loves to be fed, that has to be fed.

John Calipari during Kentucky's NCAA matchup with Iowa State.
Mark Cornelison | Lexington Herald-Leader

John Calipari talked with Doron Lamb and Michael Kidd-Gilchrist during UK's loss to Indiana in December.
Mark Cornelison | Lexington Herald-Leader

He is the master marketer. Calipari has CoachCal.com and a never-ending array of tweets. He has Orange Leaf and coaching clinics and Pro Camps, and he even coached the Dominican Republic National Team this summer.

No, check that. He not only coached the Dominican Republic National Team this summer, he organized and executed a pair of exhibition games that included former UK players now in the NBA, which sold out Rupp Arena. We're talking about exhibition games.

He is also a better coach than he often gets credit for. Last season's Kentucky team was 5-5 at one point in the SEC. It ended up 10-6, won the SEC Tournament, then beat top seed Ohio State in the NCAA Tournament. To get there, the coach who supposedly can't X and O, who can't win the close ones, triumphed in a slew of close games.

He did not win a close one in the Final Four, however. That's no sin, by any means. To reach the Final Four is a tremendous accomplishment for any team, for most programs.

Thing is, Kentucky isn't most programs. Getting the Cats back to the Final Four is great. It's not, however, what is expected. If you are the Kentucky coach, at some point you are expected to win a national championship.

Cal has never won one of those. He reached a Final Four at UMass way back in 1996. (He lost to UK in the national semifinals.) He reached the national finals while at Memphis, losing in overtime to Kansas. He returned to the Final Four last season, one of those rare coaches to take three different teams to the Final Four. (Spare me your "vacate" venting.)

But he hasn't stood there on Monday night with the trophy in his hand.

This year may be his best chance. As always, that may have as much to do with timing as talent. Connecticut will be good this year, as will Ohio State, Syracuse and a few others.

North Carolina will be very good, thanks to an impressive mix of talent and experience in Chapel Hill. When it's all said and done, most think the title will come down to UNC or UK come April in New Orleans.

After all, in less than three short years, John Calipari has done everything he set out to do at Kentucky.

Almost.

There's just one thing left.■

VS. INDIANA

WILDCATS 102
HOOSIERS 90

GEORGIA DOME **MARCH 23, 2012**

BY: JERRY TIPTON

NCAA TOURNAMENT: GAME 3

KENTUCKY ANSWERS EVERY CHALLENGE

Kidd-Gilchrist, Miller lead clutch Cats

Freshman Michael Kidd-Gilchrist predicted Kentucky and Indiana would stage an entertaining NCAA Tournament Sweet 16 game here Friday night.

"It'll be a fun game to watch for you all," he told reporters Thursday.

Out of the mouth of a babe and onto the Georgia Dome court.

Making those practices a month ago without Anthony Davis seem prescient, Kentucky outlasted Indiana 102-90.

Foul trouble limited Davis' usual dominating impact. But other UK players more than compensated.

Kidd-Gilchrist, who had scored 16 points in the past three games, led Kentucky with 24, which tied a career high.

"Mike's a spectacular player," Davis said. "Coach Cal told him to go out and rebound the ball. That's what he did."

Kidd-Gilchrist also made 10 of 10 free throws to lead Kentucky to a 35-for-37 performance from the foul line. That marked the program's second-best NCAA Tournament accuracy, bested only by an 18-for-18 game against Utah in 2003.

Doron Lamb scored 21 points, Darius Miller 19, Marquis Teague 14 and Terrence Jones 12.

Davis finished with nine points (snapping a streak of six straight games in double digits), 12 rebounds and three blocks.

The 102 points marked UK's most productive

Above: Michael Kidd-Gilchrist and Darius Miller celebrated UK's NCAA win over Indiana in Atlanta.
Charles Bertram | Lexington Herald-Leader

Right: Marquis Teague scored on a drive past Indiana forward Tom Pritchard in the NCAA South Regional semifinal in the Georgia Dome in Atlanta. *Charles Bertram | Lexington Herald-Leader*

KENTUCKY
25
INDIANA
25
UK

KENTUCKY
14
INDIANA
23
1
INDIANA
7:27
BASKETBALL
BALL CHAMPIONSHIPS
NCAA.com

Above: Terrence Jones and Hoosiers forward Will Sheehey scrapped for a loose ball as No. 1 Kentucky played Indiana in the NCAA Sweet 16. *Mark Cornelison | Lexington Herald-Leader*

Left: Michael Kidd-Gilchrist scored two of his 24 points against Indiana in the Sweet 16. *Mark Cornelison | Lexington Herald-Leader*

offensive night in the NCAA Tournament since a 110-72 victory over San Jose State in 1996.

Kentucky (35-2) advanced to Sunday's South Regional finals. The Cats will play Baylor at 2:20 p.m. for a berth in the Final Four.

"It was a war," Calipari said of Friday's game.

When asked whether it took too much out of Kentucky, Calipari said, "When you're playing at this time of year, you have more energy than you need."

Indiana finished its return-to-prominence season with a 27-9 record.

"There's always sadness, tremendous sadness," IU Coach Tom Crean said, "and it hits you later on. There's a lot more sadness when your team and players realize they had something left (to give). The Indiana men, quote me, the Indiana men, the mighty men, they gave it all. They left it all on that court."

Christian Watford, whose three-pointer at the buzzer beat Kentucky in December, led Indiana with 27 points. Cody Zeller added 20.

When asked whether he could have imagined losing a game in which his team made 52.2 percent of its shots, Crean said, "I wouldn't imagine a free-throw discrepancy of 20."

Given Kentucky's ballyhooed roster of NBA prospects, it seemed fitting that Davis spent much of the first half between two pros.

Unfortunately for UK, those NBA types were assistant coaches Kenny Payne and Rod Strickland.

Davis sat out the final 14:05 of the first half after picking up two early fouls. That made UK's 50-47 halftime lead look huge.

When asked about practicing without Davis, Calipari said, "I think it helped us; I think it helped us coaches. If you're in panic mode, they can feel it."

It helped Kentucky's cause that Zeller got hit with two fouls in a seven-second span. That sent him to the bench for much of the final 13:23.

Other Cats picked up the slack as evidenced by UK's highest-scoring first half since a 52-25 romp at South Carolina on Feb. 4.

Jones and Kidd-Gilchrist led the way. Jones, who matched his two baskets at Indiana in the game's first 62 seconds, led the Cats with 12 first-half points. Kidd-Gilchrist added 11, including a three-point play with 49.1 seconds left that broke a 45-45 tie.

Indiana went to Zeller early in a naked attempt to again get Davis in foul trouble. As in Bloomington, it worked. Davis looked puzzled when he picked up his first foul for jockeying in the post with Zeller 24 seconds after the tip.

Although Zeller contorted his body more than once in an attempt to draw another foul on Davis, it didn't come until the 14:05 mark. Davis got the foul for trying to contest Victor Oladipo's layup attempt. Deuces were wild for Davis, who exited with two points, two rebounds and two blocks, as well as two fouls.

"My teammates told me I was fine," Davis said. "... I came out in the second half with the same intensity I planned to come out in the first half."

Those fouls dulled the excitement of Jones' start. He swished a three-pointer to begin the scoring, then hit a jumper from the left side.

Making seven of its first 10 shots, Kentucky zipped to a 16-11 lead.

The margin grew to as much as 31-22 when UK answered Watford's first basket five seconds later with Jones' fast-break dunk off a lob from Teague.

That prompted an Indiana timeout with 9:55 left in the half and the reinsertion of Zeller into the game. The Hoosiers went immediately to Zeller, who made two free throws to slow UK's momentum.

Watford took over from there, scoring 15 points inside the final six minutes. His drive gave IU its largest lead of the first half, 43-39, with 3:30 left.

Jones picked up his third foul at the 17:57 mark of the second half. Miller quelled any anxiety by hitting a pair of three-pointers while scoring eight straight points. Each of his threes led to an eight-point lead for Kentucky.

But Indiana wouldn't go down easily. Four times, UK took eight-point leads before the margin grew to double digits. Davis, who was fouled on a fourth-chance opportunity, made two free throws to put the Cats ahead 74-64 with 10:26 left.

Offensive rebounding paid off big for Kentucky. Putbacks by Kidd-Gilchrist and Davis widened the margin to 79-66 with 8:57 left.

Indiana, which squandered a nine-point lead in the final eight minutes against UK in Bloomington, mounted the rally this time. Watford and Zeller brought the Hoosiers within five, 82-77. More than five minutes remained.

But two Lamb free throws and a drive by Miller pointed Kentucky toward a hard-earned victory.■

Marquis Teague scored on an easy layup in Kentucky's 102-90 win over Indiana. *Mark Cornelison | Lexington Herald-Leader*

KENTUCKY
25
WELCOME TO THE NCAA BASKETBALL CHAMPIONSHIPS
NCAA.com
1:12
UK
INDIANA
1
KENTUCKY
23
INDIANA

BY: JOHN CLAY

CATS, HOOSIERS DELIVER CLASSIC

Not even Indiana's best can dent Kentucky's armor

These Kentucky Wildcats may go on and win three more games, capture the national championship and hang an eighth banner in Rupp Arena.

But they may not play a better, more exciting, more entertaining game than the one Friday night in the Georgia Dome that was the South Regional semifinal and a 102-90 Kentucky victory over Indiana.

"It was a war," said Kentucky Coach John Calipari. "Indiana played great and we just happened to play a little bit better."

And Cal also said this: "I love coaching this type of game."

This one was old school, in the best sense of the word. Add another memorable one to the Kentucky-Indiana list.

In a college game that has grown increasingly slow and low-scoring, this one had fast breaks and bundles of baskets.

Praise Michael Kidd-Gilchrist, the furious freshman who promised the Cats would administer some payback. The New Jersey native did more than even the box score showed with his 24 points and 10 rebounds. He was a perfect 10-of-10 from the foul line.

"Mike," said teammate Anthony Davis, "is a spectacular player."

Praise Doron Lamb, the sophomore who scored 21 points, hitting eight straight free throws.

Praise Darius Miller, the senior, who scored 19 points off the bench, hitting six of eight field goals, both of his three-point attempts and all five of his free throws.

"The game was a very intense game, it was up-and-down for the most part," Miller said. "It was a fun game to be a part of, the way both teams played."

"That was a hard-fought battle," said Indiana Coach Tom Crean. "I'm looking at the stat sheet trying to figure it out and I guess the biggest thing is the fouls and when they got to the bonus."

That was the thing, on a night when everything was fast and furious, tense and traumatic, Kentucky calmly made 35 of 37 free throws. At one point, the Cats made 17 straight.

"They're great drivers," said Indiana center Cody

Above: Terrence Jones blocked Indiana guard Jordan Hulls as Kentucky cruised to a Sweet 16 win in the Georgia Dome. *Mark Cornelison | Lexington Herald-Leader*

Below: Darius Miller and Michael Kidd-Gilchrist celebrated Kentucky's Sweet 16 win, which avenged an early-season defeat to Indiana. *Mark Cornelison | Lexington Herald-Leader*

Anthony Davis blocked a shot by Indiana forward Cody Zeller in the second half of Kentucky's 102-90 win in the NCAA South Regional semifinal in the Georgia Dome.
Charles Bertram | Lexington Herald-Leader

BOX SCORE

INDIANA

## Player Name	TOT-FG FG-FGA	3-PT FG-FGA	FT-FTA	REBOUNDS OF	DE	TOT	PF	TP	A	TO	BLK	S	MIN
02 Watford, Christian.. f	9-20	3-9	6-8	0	5	5	4	27	2	1	2	1	36
10 Sheehey, Will....... f	5-8	0-1	0-0	2	2	4	5	10	0	1	0	1	35
40 Zeller, Cody........ c	9-14	0-0	2-2	3	4	7	3	20	2	3	0	0	27
01 Hulls, Jordan....... g	5-12	2-4	0-0	1	2	3	3	12	9	0	0	1	33
04 Oladipo, Victor..... g	6-8	0-1	3-4	0	2	2	5	15	3	1	0	0	20
11 Moore, Daniel.......	0-0	0-0	0-0	0	0	0	2	0	0	0	0	0	0+
23 Abell, Remy.........	2-3	0-1	2-2	0	1	1	2	6	0	2	0	0	14
25 Pritchard, Tom......	0-2	0-0	0-0	3	0	3	2	0	0	0	0	0	13
30 Roth, Matt..........	0-2	0-2	0-0	0	0	0	0	0	0	0	0	0	14
32 Elston, Derek.......	0-0	0-0	0-1	0	3	3	1	0	0	0	0	0	8
TEAM................				3		3							
Totals.............	36-69	5-18	13-17	12	19	31	27	90	16	8	2	3	200

TOTAL FG%	1st Half:	18-31 58.1%	2nd Half:	18-38 47.4%	Game:	52.2%	DEADB
3-Pt. FG%	1st Half:	2-7 28.6%	2nd Half:	3-11 27.3%	Game:	27.8%	REBS
F Throw %	1st Half:	9-13 69.2%	2nd Half:	4-4 100 %	Game:	76.5%	1

KENTUCKY

## Player Name	TOT-FG FG-FGA	3-PT FG-FGA	FT-FTA	REBOUNDS OF	DE	TOT	PF	TP	A	TO	BLK	S	MIN
03 Jones, Terrence..... f	5-9	1-2	1-2	3	2	5	3	12	0	1	1	1	27
14 Kidd-Gilchrist, M... f	7-15	0-1	10-10	6	4	10	2	24	1	2	0	0	34
23 Davis, Anthony...... c	2-5	0-1	5-6	2	10	12	2	9	2	0	3	0	25
20 Lamb, Doron......... g	6-10	1-1	8-8	0	3	3	2	21	2	1	0	1	38
25 Teague, Marquis..... g	4-14	0-2	6-6	0	3	3	3	14	7	2	0	1	36
01 Miller, Darius......	6-8	2-2	5-5	2	1	3	4	19	0	0	0	0	32
10 Beckham, Twany......	0-0	0-0	0-0	0	0	0	0	0	0	0	0	0	0+
30 Vargas, Eloy........	0-1	0-0	0-0	1	0	1	1	0	0	0	0	0	2
33 Wiltjer, Kyle.......	1-2	1-1	0-0	0	0	0	1	3	0	0	0	0	6
TEAM................				1	1	2							
Totals.............	31-64	5-10	35-37	15	24	39	18	102	12	6	4	3	200

TOTAL FG%	1st Half:	19-39 48.7%	2nd Half:	12-25 48.0%	Game:	48.4%	DEADB
3-Pt. FG%	1st Half:	3-7 42.9%	2nd Half:	2-3 66.7%	Game:	50.0%	REBS
F Throw %	1st Half:	9-10 90.0%	2nd Half:	26-27 96.3%	Game:	94.6%	1

Officials: Mark Whitehead, Ed Corbett, Ray Natili

Technical fouls: Indiana — None. Kentucky — None.

Attendance: 24,731

Score by Periods	1st	2nd	Total
Indiana	47	43	90
Kentucky	50	52	102

Zeller. "They got to the bonus early and once they got there, they were knocking them down."

Kentucky did a good portion of this without the National Player of the Year, Anthony Davis, for 14 minutes of a 20-minute first half.

Davis picked up his second foul with 14:05 left in the first half, and he viewed the remainder of the action from the Kentuckybench.

Yet, Kentucky led 50-47 at the half, even though Indiana shot 58.1 percent.

To have a great game, you must have two great teams. Indiana may not be quite great, but the Hoosiers shot 52.2 percent.

That snapped a streak of 69 straight games in which Calipari's club had held an opponent under 50 percent from the floor.

"That was them," Miller said. "I don't think we lacked intensity or focus, they just did a great job with their game plan, coming out to play."

Christian Watford, he of the buzzer-beater that conquered the Cats in December in Bloomington, scored a game-high 27 points. Zeller, who fought foul trouble of his own in the first half, scored 20.

If some thought UK would easily exact revenge for that lone regular-season loss, Crean wasn't about to let that happen.

The Hoosiers played rough and tough, but when Zeller scored the opening basket of the second half to pull Indiana to within 50-49, Crean's team could draw no closer.

"We were playing uphill," Crean said, "but it was never out of reach."

And Crean said this: "The Indiana mighty men gave it all. When you give every ounce that you have, you can move forward. And that's where we're at."

Kentucky moves forward to a 2:20 p.m. Sunday date with Baylor, which beat Xavier 75-70 in Friday night's first semifinal here.

"They are some hard-nosed young men," said Crean of the Cats, then added of his friend: "They are extremely well-coached. He's a great coach."

And this was a great game.■

VS. BAYLOR

WILDCATS 82
BEARS 70

GEORGIA DOME — **MARCH 25, 2012**

BY: JERRY TIPTON — NCAA TOURNAMENT: GAME 4

BEAR FACTS: 'WE LOST TO A GOLIATH'

Fast breaks nullify Baylor's zone

Except for freshman sensation Anthony Davis crumbling to the floor and clutching his left knee, Kentucky's advance to this year's Final Four Sunday held little suspense.

The Cats cruised past Baylor 82-70 in the South Regional finals.

"We lost to a Goliath," Baylor guard Brady Heslip said of UK. "They're No. 1 for a reason. They showed it."

Davis, who blocked six shots to give him 175 for the season, breaking the Southeastern Conference single-season record (170 by Mississippi State's Jarvis Varnado in 2008-09 and 2009-10), hurt his knee early in the second half.

Suddenly, chasing the NCAA record for blocks in a season by a freshman (he got to within eight by game's end), not to mention Kentucky's national semifinal game against archrival Louisville, receded in significance.

Davis, who scored 18 points and grabbed 11 rebounds, sprawled to the floor after colliding with Baylor's Perry Jones III with 18:38 left in the second half. After several quiet minutes on the floor, Davis made his way to the UK bench where he grimaced as trainer Chris Simmons worked on his knee.

"You just bumped it, right?" said walk-on Sam Malone, who sat next to Davis. "You didn't hurt it."

Davis' nod affirmed Malone's belief that Kentucky could proceed intact to a second straight Final Four.

"As soon as he went down, I saw the other kid holding his knee," Malone said of his suspicion that the players merely bumped knees. "It kind of made sense. I didn't get too scared."

Above: Forward Terrence Jones pulled down a rebound against Baylor in the Georgia Dome. *Mark Cornelison | Lexington Herald-Leader*

Right: Anthony Davis fought to keep the ball away from Baylor forward Perry Jones III in the second half. UK won 82-70. *Charles Bertram | Lexington Herald-Leader*

KENTUCKY
23
KENTUCKY
20

Kentucky (36-2) achieved a 36th victory in a season for only the second time in program history. The Fabulous Five went 36-3 in winning the 1947-48 national championship.

Baylor (30-8) came into the game billed as a threat because of its length and athleticism, particularly when used in a 1-3-1 zone.

But those attributes never materialized as Kentucky sped to transition scores before Baylor could set its defense.

"Impossible to guard in transition," Baylor Coach Scott Drew said of Kentucky. "Impossible."

After a settling-in period, Kentucky used a 33-7 run to build a 40-18 lead in a first half that saw UK ahead 42-22 at intermission. Kentucky scored 13 of its first 30 points on the fast break. The chief beneficiary was Michael Kidd-Gilchrist, who scored 17 of his team-high 19 points in the first half.

"Just turnovers," Heslip said in explaining Kentucky's smothering first-half dominance. "Turnovers converted into baskets for them at the other end. We weren't taking shots we normally take. We were forcing it, getting into the lane. With those trees in there, you can't really do that."

As an unneeded but welcome bonus, Kentucky's jump shooting made Baylor's half-court set defense irrelevant. During its breakout run (or for a period of about 10 minutes), UK did not miss a jump shot.

Kentucky got either a basket or free-throw attempts on 12 straight trips down court. That efficiency enabled UK to erase its last deficit (10-7) on a Marquis Teague three-pointer and assume a 32-17 lead (on a pull-up jumper in the lane by Kidd-Gilchrist).

"They're along the lines of Missouri in terms of transition (offense)," Baylor's Quincy Acy said of the Cats. "Except they're big. That's hard to stop."

Kentucky's defense befuddled Baylor. The Bears made only three of their final 20 shots of the half. Jones III, who is projected high in the various NBA mock drafts, made one of five shots, scoring two points and committing three turnovers in the half.

Marquis Teague drove past Baylor guard Deuce Bello in the NCAA South Regional final in the Georgia Dome in Atlanta. *Charles Bertram | Lexington Herald-Leader*

WELCOME TO THE NCAA BASKETBALL CHAMPIONSH
KENTUCKY
BAYLOR
22
KENTUCKY
1
WOMEN

"It was like we didn't have that fight in us," he said.

The opening minutes promised a competitive game. With Davis missing a dunk and Baylor making four of its first five shots,Kentucky fell behind 10-5.

Barely 12 minutes later, Kentucky led 38-17.

Kentucky got its scare when Davis went down with 18:38 left. As he rose for a shot off a drive, Davis got bumped by Jones III. The contact, though seemingly not extraordinary, knocked Davis off balance and to the floor.

Davis stayed down along the baseline near the basket as Jones got up slowly and went to the Baylor bench under assistance.

"I wasn't concerned," Davis said. "I was just in a lot of pain. I just had to walk it off."

As the trainer worked on Davis, UK Coach John Calipari's bedside manner tended more toward wishful thinking/risk avoidance.

"Coach Cal said, 'Stop playing, get up,'" Davis said with a smile. "I was in real pain."

An assuring round of applause erupted as Davis got off the bench with 17:31 left and walked gingerly to the scorer's table. He re-entered the game with 17:24 left and Kentucky ahead 46-28.

Thereafter, he scored four points, grabbed four rebounds and blocked four shots.

Michael Kidd-Gilchrist put in two of his 19 points against Baylor in the NCAA Elite Eight. *Mark Cornelison | Lexington Herald-Leader*

Kentucky led by as much as 23 points early in the second half.

Baylor twice closed within 13, the second time when its three-point shooter, Heslip, made his only trey. It reduced UK's lead to 63-50 with 8:52 left.

A telling moment arrived shortly thereafter. Baylor guard Pierre Jackson, who had been part of eight game-tying or clinching plays earlier this season, missed in the lane. UK's ensuing fast break yielded a driving layup by Kidd-Gilchrist.

Baylor got as close as 78-68 in the final minute.■

Left: Anthony Davis put up a shot over Baylor forward Quincy Acy during Kentucky's win in the NCAA Elite Eight. *Mark Cornelison | Lexington Herald-Leader*

Below: Michael Kidd-Gilchrist and Darius Miller celebrated Kentucky's return to the Final Four and the team's win over Baylor. *Mark Cornelison | Lexington Herald-Leader*

BIG-GAME MIKE STRIKES AGAIN

Kidd-Gilchrist shines brightest when needed most

To say Game On to the wildest sports week any Kentuckian is apt to ever experience, there was a small detail that had to be handled first.

For there to be Kentucky vs. Louisville in the Final Four, there had to be Kentucky over Baylor in the NCAA Tournament South Regional finals.

So Michael Kidd-Gilchrist took care of it.

MKG scored 17 points in a 10:08 stretch of the first half to ignite a 37-12 UK blitzkrieg to end the first half. That first-half scoring rampage allowed the Cats (36-2) to score an 82-70 victory Sunday over Baylor (30-8) before 24,035 in the NCAA Tournament round of eight.

"I've never played better than that," Kidd-Gilchrist said of the 10-minute stretch when he electrified the Georgia Dome. "I was in the zone."

Actually he was in the open court. Over and over. And once there, he was lethal.

When Baylor's Quincy Miller made a three-pointer from the top of the key with 16:45 left in half one, the Bears led 10-5. It was the biggest deficit UK had yet faced in the NCAA Tournament.

So MKG went to work.

At 15:11, he muscled in a tough 4-footer. At 12:24, he dropped in a layup. He went coast-to-coast for another layup at 11:31. Kidd-Gilchrist threw down a dunk at 10:58.

Next, he drained a three from the right wing at 9:15. At 6:42, he hit a contested 6-footer in the lane.

The 6-foot-7, 232-pound freshman from Somerdale, N.J., finished up his scoring binge with two sets of two free throws at 5:25 and 5:03.

By that time, UK led 38-17 (other Kentucky players were scoring, too).

Though Baylor showed some second-half fight — and UK got a brief scare when Anthony Davis went down after banging knees with Perry Jones

III — UK's 15th all-time Final Four bid was essentially secured by the end of Kidd-Gilchrist's surge.

"Mike had a lot of success out in transition, and we just kept feeding him," Kentucky point guard Marquis Teague said.

Said UK power forward Terrence Jones: "When I see Michael running, I believe something good is going to happen."

For one so young, Kidd-Gilchrist - who fouled out with 19 points and five rebounds — has shown a remarkable capacity to impose his will on the biggest of games.

MKG hit North Carolina for 17 points and 11 boards. He had 18 and nine at Indiana. Against Louisville in Rupp Arena, he went for 24 and 19.

"He wants to win so bad, he just does whatever it takes," said Teague of Kidd-Gilchrist.

Said UK swingman Darius Miller: "Mike is one of the most competitive people I've ever played with."

In Atlanta for the South Regional, Kidd-Gilchrist snapped out of a recent scoring slump, having failed to score in double figures in seven of 11 games.

Against IU in the round of 16, Kidd-Gilchrist burned the Hoosiers for 24 points and 10 rebounds. Then he did in Baylor with his one-man, first-half transition game.

There was exactly zero shock value when MKG was named South Regional MOP — Most Outstanding Player.

"A great feeling," Kidd-Gilchrist said of the honor. "But I'm not done yet. On to the next game."

It is definitely on.

For the first time ever, it's UK vs. U of L in the Final Four.

Louisville fans can draw strength from some numbers.

While John Calipari and Rick Pitino are 8-8 against each other as college head coaches, Pitino is 4-0 vs. Cal in post-season tournament contests (2-0 in NCAA tourneys when Ricky P. was at UK and Cal at Massachusetts; 2-0 in Conference USA Tournaments when Pitino was at U of L and Calipari at Memphis).

The last four Kentucky seasons have ended with a tournament (NCAA or NIT) loss to a Big East foe. Louisville is in the Big East.

Kentucky fans can draw strength from some facts.

BOX SCORE

BAYLOR

	TOT-FG	3-PT		REBOUNDS									
## Player Name	FG-FGA	FG-FGA	FT-FTA	OF	DE	TOT	PF	TP	A	TO	BLK	S	MIN
04 Acy, Quincy......... f	7-11	0-0	8-8	3	5	8	3	22	1	3	2	1	34
30 Miller, Quincy...... f	1-6	1-2	0-0	0	6	6	3	3	1	1	2	0	19
01 Jones III, Perry.... c	6-14	1-2	4-5	3	5	8	4	17	2	4	0	0	34
05 Heslip, Brady....... g	1-2	1-2	1-2	0	1	1	4	4	1	0	0	0	26
55 Jackson, Pierre..... g	9-19	1-7	2-2	2	0	2	4	21	5	4	0	2	38
00 Franklin, Gary......	0-1	0-0	0-0	0	0	0	5	0	3	0	1	0	9
03 Ellis, Fred.........	0-0	0-0	0-0	0	0	0	1	0	0	0	0	0	1
14 Bello, Deuce........	1-3	0-0	1-2	0	1	1	3	3	0	1	0	2	13
22 Walton, A.J.........	0-4	0-1	0-0	1	0	1	4	0	2	1	0	0	19
41 Jones, Anthony......	0-4	0-0	0-0	2	0	2	1	0	0	0	0	0	7
Team................				5		5							
Totals.............	25-64	4-14	16-19	16	18	34	32	70	15	14	5	5	200

TOTAL FG%	1st Half:	8-25 32.0%	2nd Half:	17-39 43.6%	Game:	39.1%	DEADB
3-Pt. FG%	1st Half:	1-4 25.0%	2nd Half:	3-10 30.0%	Game:	28.6%	REBS
F Throw %	1st Half:	5-6 83.3%	2nd Half:	11-13 84.6%	Game:	84.2%	2

KENTUCKY

	TOT-FG	3-PT		REBOUNDS									
## Player Name	FG-FGA	FG-FGA	FT-FTA	OF	DE	TOT	PF	TP	A	TO	BLK	S	MIN
03 Jones, Terrence..... f	3-7	0-1	6-12	2	7	9	1	12	6	2	3	2	35
14 Kidd-Gilchrist, M... f	7-10	1-1	4-4	2	3	5	5	19	1	3	0	0	27
23 Davis, Anthony...... c	6-9	0-0	6-8	3	8	11	4	18	1	0	6	2	32
20 Lamb, Doron......... g	3-7	1-3	7-12	0	1	1	2	14	1	2	0	2	32
25 Teague, Marquis..... g	2-4	1-1	3-4	0	3	3	3	8	3	4	0	1	30
01 Miller, Darius......	2-6	0-2	4-4	0	0	0	2	8	3	1	0	2	35
30 Vargas, Eloy........	0-0	0-0	0-0	0	0	0	0	0	0	0	0	0	2
33 Wiltjer, Kyle.......	1-2	1-1	0-0	0	0	0	1	3	0	0	0	0	7
TEAM................				1	2	3				1			
Totals.............	24-45	4-9	30-44	8	24	32	18	82	15	13	9	9	200

TOTAL FG%	1st Half:	16-29 55.2%	2nd Half:	8-16 50.0%	Game:	53.3%	DEADB
3-Pt. FG%	1st Half:	3-6 50.0%	2nd Half:	1-3 33.3%	Game:	44.4%	REBS
F Throw %	1st Half:	7-10 70.0%	2nd Half:	23-34 67.6%	Game:	68.2%	9

Officials: Les Jones, Bryan Kersey, Mike Stuart

Technical fouls: Baylor — None. Kentucky — None.

Attendance: 24,035

Score by Periods	1st	2nd	Total
Baylor	22	48	70
Kentucky	42	40	82

Louisville shot 32.3 percent in its 69-62 loss to Kentucky in Rupp Arena on Dec. 31. Other than Russ Smith, the Cards were really bothered by UK's defensive length.

The Cats have not gotten any smaller since New Year's Eve.

Kentucky just has more talent. At nbadraft.net, there are six Wildcats projected to be taken in the first 44 picks of the 2012 NBA Draft. There are no Louisville players on the mock-draft list.

In our state, games won't get much bigger than Kentucky-Louisville in the Final Four.

Which means UK will have one other advantage, too: It has Big-Game Mike.

"I wish we could play right now," Kidd-Gilchrist said. "I can't wait."■

Left: Kentucky players celebrated with the trophy after defeating Baylor in the NCAA South Regional final in the Georgia Dome. UK moved on to the Final Four with the 82-70 win. *Charles Bertram | Lexington Herald-Leader*

VS. LOUISVILLE

WILDCATS	69
CARDINALS	61

MERCEDES-BENZ SUPERDOME MARCH 31, 2012

BY: JERRY TIPTON NCAA TOURNAMENT: GAME 5

BEST IN TENSION: UK COMES THROUGH

Cats too clutch for Louisville down stretch

With archrival Louisville largely succeeding in keeping it close and thereby turning up the pressure, Kentucky proved its championship mettle again Saturday. Now, the Cats have only to beat Kansas on Monday night to be champions in name, as well as spirit.

Kentucky outlasted Louisville 69-61 in the NCAA Tournament national semifinals. As U of L intended, it wasn't easy. But UK was up to the task.

"Whoever wins the Kansas-Ohio State game is going to have to play a hell of a game to beat them," Louisville Coach Rick Pitino said in tribute to the Cats.

UK, which set a school record with its 37th victory, had to win it in the final nine minutes. Claims of just another opponent aside, Doron Lamb acknowledged that the Cats felt how desperately the Big Blue Nation wanted — needed — this victory.

"I'm sick of that," he said of UK-U of L. "I'm glad it's over. It was pressure. (UK fans) would have really hated it if we lost to them."

Still, Kentucky did not tremble when Louisville's steady uphill climb crested at 49-49.

"We just needed a lot of things to go right," Pitino said.

Kentucky needed to be Kentucky.

"I have a team that's had (opponents) come at them all year," UK Coach John Calipari said, "and they've responded like they did today."

Above: Michael Kidd-Gilchrist and Louisville's Peyton Siva battled for the ball in the first half in New Orleans. *Mark Cornelison | Lexington Herald-Leader*

Right: Doron Lamb, Michael Kidd-Gilchrist and Marquis Teague celebrated Kentucky's 69-61 Final Four win over Louisville in New Orleans. *Mark Cornelison | Lexington Herald-Leader*

KENTUCKY
1
SIVA
3
5

Above: Marquis Teague fought for the ball against Louisville's Russ Smith (2) and Chris Smith (5) in the Final Four.
Mark Cornelison | Lexington Herald-Leader

Left: Darius Miller looked to pass as Chris Smith and Peyton Siva applied pressure in the semifinal game of the NCAA Final Four in New Orleans. *Charles Bertram | Lexington Herald-Leader*

Louisville set the stage by rallying from a 10-point deficit to tie it at 49 with nine minutes left. Anybody's ball game.

Anthony Davis loomed large in tying DeMarcus Cousins' school freshman record for double-doubles with 20. His 18 points and 14 rebounds led UK. He also blocked five shots to increase his season total to 180, two shy of the NCAA record for a freshman (Hassan Whiteside of Marshall in 2009-10).

Darius Miller's 13 points included a clutch three-pointer down the stretch. Lamb added 10.

Louisville (30-10) was led by Peyton Siva's 11 points. Chane Behanan added 10 points and nine rebounds.

Kentucky led 35-28 at halftime. That represented an effective holding action by Louisville, which teetered on the edge of a first-half knockout.

Louisville made only five of its first 21 shots. That included missed dunks by Behanan and center Gorgui Dieng.

U of L stayed close by outrebounding UK 40-33 for the game and limiting transition play.

Never trailing but never comfortably ahead in the final 39 minutes, Kentucky made its first four shots to zip to an 8-2 lead.

Needing any transition points in a poor-shooting game, Louisville got two when Chris Smith stole Lamb's pass and sped to a fast-break layup. That reduced UK's lead to 26-20 and prompted a timeout with 3:41 left.

Louisville, which made seven of its final 11 shots in the half, got as close as 31-28. Dieng took a behind-the-back pass from Chris Smith and dunked while being fouled by Miller.

The Cards got no closer before halftime, but Louisville had Kentucky's attention.

When U of L fouled with 2:21 left, UK only got to take the ball out, and Calipari turned to his assistants to say, "Are we shooting (the one-and-one) yet?"

No, it was only Louisville's fourth foul, which indicated that the Cards had succeeded in limiting Kentucky's free-throw opportunities. U of L didn't commit a foul until the 9:58 mark. UK made four of five free throws in the first half, a huge difference from the 32-for-43 parade that beat Louisville on New Year's Eve. In that game, the Cats made 17 of 23 foul shots in the first half alone.

Kentucky re-established control early in the second half. Miller led the way, scoring easily on a turnaround over Siva and then stealing Behanan's lazy pass and breezing to a transition dunk. The latter put UK ahead 43-32, prompting a U of L time out with 16:44 left.

Marquis Teague went to the basket against Louisville's Gorgui Dieng in the NCAA Final Four. *Mark Cornelison | Lexington Herald-Leader*

The lead grew to as much as 13, and UK matched its first-half free-throw total inside the first eight minutes, but Louisville rallied. Rebounding sparked the counter-surge as the Cardinals outrebounded UK 15-4 in the first eight minutes of the second half.

Put-back dunks by Dieng and Wayne Blackshear reduced Kentucky's lead to 46-42 with 11:23 left.

Siva's first basket — a three-pointer from the top of the key — brought U of L all the way back, tying it at 49. More than nine minutes remained. In that time, Louisville made only four of 15 shots.

Back-to-back baskets by Michael Kidd-Gilchrist steadied UK. On the second, he drove the middle of the lane, spun 360 degrees and slammed home a dunk to put the Cats ahead 53-49.

The margin grew to 60-51 when Miller hit a transition three-pointer and then two free throws after being fouled on a drive. Less than five minutes stood between Kentucky and a date in Monday's championship game.

"I didn't feel any pressure at all," Kidd-Gilchrist said. "None at all."

Nor did he sound concerned with Monday night's championship game.

Of adding to Kentucky's seven national championships, Kidd-Gilchrist told reporters, "No. 8 is on the way."■

Anthony Davis blocked a shot by Louisville's Peyton Siva. *Mark Cornelison | Lexington Herald-Leader*

BY: JOHN CLAY

MILLER MAKES MOST OF MOMENT

Kentuckian steps into a shot, into a hug and into the title game

All game long, John Calipari had been riding his in-state senior.

Nothing new there. Cal was yelling. Cal was pleading. Cal was all up in Darius Miller, telling him to rebound, to defend, to stop falling away on his shot.

But now, after Louisville had rallied to tie the score with 9:11 remaining, and Kentucky had squirmed back in front by a couple of baskets, surely the Cats needed something extra to squeeze out some separation.

Then, there it was, Kentucky turning a Louisville miss into a fast break, point guard Marquis Teague roaring down the floor with the basketball, sensing a familiar presence from behind just in time to feed his trailing teammate.

This time, Miller didn't fade. He rose. He shot. He stepped right into it. He knocked it down.

It made the score 58-51 Kentucky with five minutes remaining as Rick Pitino's head dropped down, the Louisville coach asking for a timeout.

Before Miller could even get to the bench, there was his head coach, up in his face again, only this time with a smile. Miller answered with a hug.

"I don't know if he hugged me," Calipari said, "but I know I hugged him."

At that point, you just knew that Kentucky was going to win this game, that Kentucky was going to its first national championship game since 1998.

And so it is: Cats 69, Cards 61.

"It was," said Miller afterward, "an emotional game."

Yes, Anthony Davis showed why he is the national player of the year, scoring 18 points and grabbing 14 rebounds.

Darius Miller fought for a rebound late in the game against Louisville. *Charles Bertram | Lexington Herald-Leader*

Michael Kidd-Gilchrist scored key baskets to start the deciding run. Terrence Jones appeared out of the clouds late to grab rebounds and throw down baskets.

But it was that Miller Moment that put the stamp on this Dream Game II, Final Four version, with Kentucky Blue and Louisville Red flooding Bourbon Street.

The game itself may not have matched the hype. It may not have been terribly well played. It may not have been spine-tingling. It may not have been dramatic.

But for the winners, the tournament's overall No. 1 seed, it was a must-win, not just to beat the archrival 80 miles down the road, but to advance one game beyond last season.

"I don't think we felt the pressure," Jones said. "But I know we wanted to win."

And survive.

Calipari paced the sideline of the raised court — his stool nothing more than a prop — jumped and twirled and danced.

Late, when the contest was still hanging in the balance, there was Davis uncharacteristically pointing and yelling during a timeout, thumping his chest to the point where he had to be all but tackled by a teammate.

"We wanted this game," said Doron Lamb.

Louisville wanted it, too. Make no mistake. Rick Pitino is still Rick Pitino. Give him five long days to prepare and he will have his team knowing everything there is to know about your team. Kentucky shot 60 percent the first half, yet led by just three, 31-28, with 1:30 left when Gorgui Dieng completed an old-fashioned three-point play.

Even when a Kyle Wiltjer three-pointer helped extend the margin to seven at the half, 35-28, Louisville did what it did in Lexington back on Dec. 31.

Down 15 in the first half then, the Cards tied the game at 40. Down by 11 at 45-34 in this game, the Cards rallied to tie it at 49.

Moments later, there was the Miller hug. And more. After the timeout, with 5:04 left, U of L missed a shot in traffic. Quickly, there was Miller getting fouled at the other end, then sinking the free throws for a nine-point Kentucky lead.

It was finally breathing room in a week where the fans on both sides had surely found it hard to breathe.

"We played good," said Calipari afterward. "We didn't play our best."

They hope their best comes Monday. This is a business trip, after all. That's been this young but mature team's mantra.

They can always come back to New Orleans. They'd rather leave as champions.

Monday night they want to close the deal on a season and bring home a banner. But they had to win this game first, with all its hype, and buildup, and passion.

"I'm sure they really wanted it really bad, with it being Louisville," Miller, the man from Maysville, was saying afterward of his team's fans. "(But) our main goal is to win a championship, not beat a certain team."

True, but on this day, in this game, they did have to beat a certain team, one from the same state.

They had to step into it, and knock 'em down.

Helped by the in-state senior, that's exactly what they did.■

Michael Kidd-Gilchrist shouted after dunking in the second half against Louisville.
Charles Bertram | Lexington Herald-Leader

NCAA.com
2012 NCAA FINAL FOUR
KENTUCKY
KENTUCKY
MILLER
KENTUCKY

Michael Kidd-Gilchrist grabbed teammate Anthony Davis after Kentucky defeated Louisville 69-61 to move on to the NCAA title game. *Mark Cornelison | Lexington Herald-Leader*

THE CENTER OF IT ALL

Davis proves many awards deserved

Basketball fans from Kentucky filled up Bourbon Street late Friday night. Decked out in Louisville red and Kentucky blue, they yelled and they spelled.

C-A-R-D-S!

Oh yeah, well, C-A-T-S!

By Saturday evening, Kentuckians had made the Big Easy the Big Electric.

The first Final Four matchup ever between Kentucky and Louisville filled the Mercedes-Benz Superdome — a cavernous NFL stadium — to the brim.

After 38:53 seconds of grueling back-and-forth basketball, Anthony Davis did what he's done so many times in his scintillating Kentucky freshman year.

He brought the house down.

And brought Kentucky home.

Catching a deflected Michael Kidd-Gilchrist alley-oop pass, Davis snared it with one hand, appeared to readjust the path of his leap in the air and cuffed the ball emphatically into the basket.

The dunk brought an explosion of noise from the Big Blue sections of the crowd and gave UK a seven-point lead over the plucky Cards.

"It got tipped," Kentucky Coach John Calipari said later of Kidd-Gilchrist's pass. "Anthony somehow grabbed it one-hand and dunked it, and it basically ended the game."

So it did. Kentucky 69, Louisville 61.

Having dispatched their fiercest rival, UK will have a chance Monday night to claim its eighth NCAA championship and first since 1998.

As it has been so many times this year for the Cats (37-2), the primary difference between victory and defeat was Davis.

Louisville's Russ Smith tried to put up a shot between Terrence Jones and Anthony Davis. *Mark Cornelison | Lexington Herald-Leader*

The 6-foot-10 Chicago product finished with 18 points, 14 rebounds and five blocked shots. Even those impressive numbers don't reflect his full impact on the game.

Kentucky survived a determined U of L (30-10) upset bid because the Cardinals could not find the basket. A big part of the U of L offensive problem was the shot-altering impact of Davis.

For the game, Louisville made only 24 of 69 shots. The Cardinals' starting front line combined to go 10-for-27. Penetrating guards Peyton Siva, Chris Smith and Russ Smith went 11-for-37.

"Anthony Davis, he's a great player," Chris Smith said. "He can change every shot."

Said U of L forward Kyle Kuric: Davis "just has great length so he's able to alter shots. It's difficult for guards like Peyton and Russ to get a clean look like they usually do."

What made Davis' performance in NOLA on college basketball's grandest stage even more impressive is that he was set up for a comeuppance. The willowy freshman big man spent the days leading up to our state's hoops Armageddon collecting national player of the year awards from, seemingly, every organization in the country except the Daughters of the American Revolution.

He was more than eligible for the basketball version of the Heisman Trophy jinx.

Yet being guarded by another shot blocker, Louisville's 6-11 Gorgui Dieng, Davis showed his ever-expanding offensive weaponry. Repeatedly, he went to a baby hook shot over the long arms of Dieng.

"I've been working on my post moves a lot," Davis said. "They've gotten a lot better since the beginning of the year. I feel very confident now in the post."

Davis did his best work offensively early in the second half. After U of L pulled within 35-31 on a Chris Smith trey to start half two, Davis scored five of Kentucky's points in an 11-3 run that opened up a 46-34 Cats lead.

After U of L, boosted by relentless work on the offensive glass, tied the game at 49, Davis found Kidd- Gilchrist with a nifty pass that led to the dunk that put UK ahead for good.

U of L gave a spirited account of itself. The same Cardinals who were outrebounded 57-31 in Rupp Arena in UK's New Year's Eve victory had a whopping 19 offensive rebounds this time and won the battle of the boards overall, 40-33.

BOX SCORE

LOUISVILLE

## Player Name	TOT-FG FG-FGA	3-PT FG-FGA	FT-FTA	REBOUNDS OF	DE	TOT	PF	TP	A	TO	BLK	S	MIN
14 Kuric, Kyle......... f	3-8	1-2	0-1	4	1	5	3	7	0	0	0	1	28
24 Behanan, Chane.... f	4-9	0-2	2-2	2	7	9	1	10	0	2	0	0	34
10 Dieng, Gorgui....... c	3-10	0-0	1-1	8	4	12	2	7	2	3	4	2	40
03 Siva, Peyton........ g	4-11	1-2	2-2	0	3	3	2	11	3	3	0	0	31
05 Smith, Chris........ g	3-11	1-2	1-2	0	1	1	1	8	1	1	0	0	23
02 Smith, Russ.........	4-15	0-1	1-2	1	2	3	2	9	1	3	0	2	26
21 Swopshire, Jared....	0-0	0-0	0-0	0	0	0	1	0	0	0	0	0	4
22 Justice, Elisha.....	0-0	0-0	0-0	0	0	0	0	0	0	0	0	0	0+
25 Blackshear, Wayne...	3-5	1-2	2-3	1	3	4	4	9	0	0	0	0	14
TEAM...............				3		3							
Totals.............	24-69	4-11	9-13	19	21	40	16	61	7	12	4	5	200

TOTAL FG%	1st Half:	12-32 37.5%	2nd Half:	12-37 32.4%	Game:	34.8%	DEADB
3-Pt. FG%	1st Half:	1-3 33.3%	2nd Half:	3-8 37.5%	Game:	36.4%	REBS
F Throw %	1st Half:	3-5 60.0%	2nd Half:	6-8 75.0%	Game:	69.2%	3

KENTUCKY

## Player Name	TOT-FG FG-FGA	3-PT FG-FGA	FT-FTA	REBOUNDS OF	DE	TOT	PF	TP	A	TO	BLK	S	MIN
03 Jones, Terrence..... f	3-8	0-0	0-3	2	5	7	2	6	0	0	2	2	33
14 Kidd-Gilchrist, M... f	4-6	0-0	1-4	0	4	4	3	9	1	4	0	0	23
23 Davis, Anthony...... f	7-8	0-0	4-6	2	12	14	2	18	2	3	5	1	39
20 Lamb, Doron......... g	4-9	0-2	2-3	0	1	1	1	10	1	4	0	0	35
25 Teague, Marquis..... g	4-8	0-0	0-0	0	2	2	4	8	5	2	0	1	33
01 Miller, Darius......	4-7	1-4	4-4	0	3	3	2	13	0	1	0	2	29
30 Vargas, Eloy........	0-0	0-0	0-0	0	0	0	0	0	0	0	0	0	0+
33 Wiltjer, Kyle.......	2-3	1-1	0-0	1	0	1	0	5	0	0	0	1	8
TEAM...............				1		1							
Totals.............	28-49	2-7	11-20	6	27	33	14	69	9	14	7	7	200

TOTAL FG%	1st Half:	15-25 60.0%	2nd Half:	13-24 54.2%	Game:	57.1%	DEADB
3-Pt. FG%	1st Half:	1-5 20.0%	2nd Half:	1-2 50.0%	Game:	28.6%	REBS
F Throw %	1st Half:	4-5 80.0%	2nd Half:	7-15 46.7%	Game:	55.0%	3

Officials: Les Jones, Doug Shows, Joe DeRosa

Technical fouls: Louisville — None. Kentucky — None.

Attendance: 24,035

Score by Periods	1st	2nd	Total
Louisville	28	33	61
Kentucky	35	34	69

Kentucky backers should shudder to think what would have happened had it not been for Davis and his 14 boards.

"That Anthony Davis is as fine a basketball player as there is," Louisville Coach Rick Pitino said.

As the Superdome game clock ticked down to 0:00, the ball, appropriately enough, ended up in the hands of Davis.

At the end of a basketball game that Kentuckians will talk about forever, as Cats fans exulted and Cards' fans despaired, Davis flung the ball high into the air and screamed, "This is my stage!"

Truer words were never spoken.■

VS. KANSAS

WILDCATS 67
JAYHAWKS 59

MERCEDES-BENZ SUPERDOME — APRIL 2, 2012

BY: JERRY TIPTON — NCAA TOURNAMENT: CHAMPIONSHIP

8TH WONDERS

Kentucky wins 8th national title, beating Kansas 67-59

Kentucky completed one of the more dominating NCAA Tournament runs in the proud program's history Monday night by beating Kansas 67-59 to claim its eighth national championship and John Calipari's first as a coach.

Ironically, Anthony Davis, who became only the fourth freshman voted the tournament's Most Outstanding Player, proved scoring can be incidental to championship play. He didn't make a basket until 5:12 left and finished with six points.

But Davis pulled down 16 rebounds, giving him 30 in the Final Four, which was the most since Hakeem Olajuwon grabbed 40 in 1983. Davis also blocked six shots, which moved his season total to 186, thus setting an NCAA record for freshmen.

When Kansas closed a nearly game-long UK lead to 65-59, Davis forced Elijah Johnson to release the ball and try to retrieve it rather than take a three-point shot. The walking call closed the deal.

Calipari saw Davis as a living example of a pointed question he asked his players a month ago: What do you do to help us win when you're not scoring the ball?

"You saw it with him," he said.

Davis' gritty production was much needed because Kansas came into the game hoping to out-tough Kentucky. No doubt, the Jayhawks hoped the muscle would work on UK's nerves.

"We're not just a talented team," Calipari said. "We're a defensive team and a team that shares the ball.

"We were the best team."

Kansas, which rallied from 13 down to beat Ohio State in Saturday's semifinals, staged one of

Above: Anthony Davis reacted after cutting down the net after the championship game. *Mark Cornelison | Lexington Herald-Leader*

Right: Marquis Teague went to the basket against Elijah Johnson (15) in the first half. *Charles Bertram | Lexington Herald-Leader*

KENTUCKY
25

JONES
3
KANSAS
0
KENTUCKY
14
UK
OHIO STATE
NCAA.com
2012 NCAA FINAL FOUR

its patented second-half comebacks. The Jayhawks reduced a onetime 18-point UK lead to 62-57 with 1:37 left.

"We got the game to what we wanted," Kansas Coach Bill Self said of the second half. "A muddy track."

Kentucky (38-2) wobbled. But the Cats showed again they could make clutch plays. With UK holding a 63-57 lead, a block by Michael Kidd-Gilchrist of a Tyshawn Taylor drive with a minute left started the celebration.

"Unbelievable play," Taylor said. "I thought I had that. ... His length is something you can't really teach."

Self saluted Kentucky.

"We came up short," he said. "But I don't think we lost."

Kentucky, which trailed for only nine minutes and eight seconds in six NCAA Tournament games, won the tournament for the first time since 1998. The eighth title leaves UK trailing only UCLA, which has won 11.

Neither Davis nor Thomas Robinson, the first consensus All-Americans to meet in a title game since Duke's Elton Brand and Connecticut's Richard Hamilton in 1999, shot well.

Terrence Jones and Anthony Davis blocked Thomas Robinson of Kansas in the NCAA title game. *Mark Cornelison | Lexington Herald-Leader*

Davis made one of 10 shots. Robinson made six of 17, while scoring 18 points and grabbing 17 rebounds.

As reflected in a 25-14 rebounding advantage, Kentucky showed plenty of toughness in the first half. The Cats added their signature transition offense to build a 41-27 halftime lead.

Although Kansas came into the championship game with a reputation for resilience and second-half comebacks, this was uncharted territory. It was the Jayhawks' largest halftime deficit of the season. The previous high came in an 87-86 overtime victory over Missouri in which Kansas trailed 44-32 at intermission.

Kentucky took the lead for good on a jumper by Marquis Teague with 16:42 left.

The Cats steadily expanded the lead, which reached its first-half zenith at 18 points twice in the final 64 seconds of the half.

Kansas came into the game ranked second (to Kentucky) in field-goal defense. But UK made 53.3 percent of its first-half shots. Baskets by Lamb and Kidd-Gilchrist gave Kentucky its 18-point margins.

Kansas suffered when Robinson made two of his first 10 shots, often missing badly. With Davis always lurking, Terrence Jones defended Robinson.

Davis, who missed his only four shots of the half, blocked three shots. The third broke the NCAA season record for freshman, which had been 182 by Marshall's Hassan Whiteside in 2009-10. Davis got the record-breaker with help defense against a posting Robinson with eight minutes left.

Kidd-Gilchrist's defense kept Taylor contained offensively.

Above: Terrence Jones drove against Thomas Robinson of the Kansas Jayhawks in the championship game. *Charles Bertram | Lexington Herald-Leader*

Left: Marquis Teague took it to the basket in the first half. *Mark Cornelison | Lexington Herald-Leader*

But back-to-back baskets by Robinson and Taylor in the final minute — the only time Kansas scored on two straight possessions in the game's first 25 minutes — reduced the UK lead to 14 at halftime.

Kansas, which had outscored its last four opponents 133-96 in the second half, closed the lead to 41-30 with 17:53 left.

Kansas was looking to come back when Robinson rebounded a Davis miss but lost the ball. That resulted in a Jones dunk, which put UK ahead 46-30, and Kansas called a timeout.

Within the next minute, Kansas scored twice in transition, prompting a UK timeout with 13:52 left.

Kansas got as close as 48-38. Then after a TV timeout, Lamb hit three-pointers from the left corner and the right wing. That put Kentucky ahead 54-38 with 10 minutes left.

With victory looking secured, there was time for levity.

After Jones missed the first of two free throws with 6:02 left, making him 0-for-9 in two Final Fours, he made the second. Calipari staggered in mock horror. A three-pointer by Taylor, which snapped personal 0-for-19 streak in domes, and 0-for-23 in the NCAA Tournament, seemed inconsequential.■

Wilson
15
KENTUCKY
1
20
KENTUCKY
14

Elijah Johnson (15) of Kansas put up a shot over Anthony Davis in the NCAA title game. *Mark Cornelison | Lexington Herald-Leader*

BY: JOHN CLAY

BLUE TOGETHER

Kentucky does it right by doing it together

"BLUE TOGETHER." Those were the words written on the grease-board John Calipari carried out with him to the floor of the NCAA Tournament national championship game Monday night at the Superdome.

Six core players, two words, one shot.

One shot to get it right.

Kentucky got it right.

By doing it right.

Kentucky 67, Kansas 59.

In the biggest game of the season, the Cats accomplished the biggest goal of the season by doing what they had done all season. This gifted team of amazing individual talent worked together, played together and shared together in a collaborative effort to win a championship.

Monday night, Anthony Davis scored all of six points and won tournament Most Outstanding Player honors. Doron Lamb pumped in 22 points, and added three assists. Terrence Jones blocked two shots. Michael Kidd-Gilchrist defended with all his might. Marquis Teague, the point guard, scored 14 points. Darius Miller, the senior, steadied the ship.

"The Road Ends Here" said the signs all over New Orleans. For this team, the road began in Lexington last summer when an ensemble cast first came together to create excellence.

They descended on campus from sea to shining sea and places in between. One kid (Lamb) from New York City. One kid (Jones) from Portland, Ore. One kid (Davis) from Chicago. One kid (Teague) from Indianapolis. One kid (Kidd-Gilchrist) from New Jersey. One kid (Miller) from Maysville, Kentucky.

Differing backgrounds, same goal. NBA-bound, yes. But championship-bound, first.

"We want to win a title," said Davis and Lamb and Kidd-Gilchrist and Jones and Teague and Miller at different points in the season.

Terrence Jones rolled his ankle in first half action in the championship game. *Charles Bertram | Lexington Herald-Leader*

Soon, egos blended into parts of equal importance. Individuality became indivisible. Star power synthesized into something special.

You could see it in Madison Square Garden when they blew away from Kansas in the second half in just the second game of the year. You could see it in the way they defeated a veteran and No. 1 North Carolina team in early December, the way they bounced back from that one-point loss at Indiana, beating Louisville, zipping through conference play undefeated.

Opponents used various styles to try to beat these Cats. Some walked. Others ran. Some played rough.

Others went finesse. Some tried to pound the paint. Others bombed away from outside. All failed to stop the blue machine.

There was pressure all season, of course, but especially here in NOLA. There was nothing easy in the Big Easy. Not when Louisville was your first hurdle. Not when a tough, disciplined, never-say-die Kansas awaited in the finals.

First half, the Cats showed their firepower. A Lamb three-pointer ended an 11-2 run and Kentucky led 34-19. It was 41-23 Cats with 1:04 left in the first half, then 41-27 at the intermission buzzer.

All without Davis, the national player of the year, scoring a point.

You knew Bill Self's team would not quit, and it did not. Inside the final four minutes, the Jayhawks sliced the margin to seven, then five at 62-57. For a brief second you had a flashback to 2008 when John Calipari and Memphis lost a nine-point lead with two minutes left and lost the title to Kansas and Self.

But then, unlike in 2008, Davis hit a free throw. Then with 53.9 seconds left, Teague hit two more, and the lead was eight.

And banner No. 8 was won.

"I don't think we lost it," Self said afterward. "I think they won it."

It's no secret these are short-timers. The purists may not like it, but we don't live in a pure world. We live in the real world. And chances are, we aren't going back. You can pine for the days when teams grew together over four years. These modern days, they must grow as one in one. One season. One shot. Make it count.

That's what they did, and when the final buzzer sounded, Calipari turned and hugged his assistants and grinned.

For once, he was speechless.

The 53-year-old veteran of four national semifinals and two title games had said it didn't matter if he won his first championship or not, it was no big deal, but you know it sure felt like a big deal.

Calipari is the one who put this team together, who molded it, directed it, guided it, taught it most importantly how to play the game the right way.

Calipari used the word drag this year, it's a favorite of his, that at first he felt like he was dragging this team forward, but in the end "carry" was the better word.

These players carried each other — to the title.

For the greatest tradition in the history of college basketball, an eighth national title was based on six core players, one goal and two words.

"BLUE TOGETHER."■

UK players during the second half.
Mark Cornelison | Lexington Herald-Leader

Wilson
KENTUCKY
23
KANSAS
5
YOUNG
40

Left: Anthony Davis went to the basket in the final game of the NCAA tournament. *Charles Bertram | Lexington Herald-Leader*

Above: Michael Kidd-Gilchrist blocked the shot of Tyshawn Taylor of Kansas late in the game. *Charles Bertram | Lexington Herald-Leader*

Upper Right: Coach John Calipari reacts in the championship game. *Charles Bertram | Lexington Herald-Leader*

Right: Michael Kidd-Gilchrist reacted after blocking a Kansas shot in second half action in the championship game. *Mark Cornelison | Lexington Herald-Leader*

Far Right: Doron Lamb reacted after making a shot in the first half of the championship game. *Mark Cornelison | Lexington Herald-Leader*

CATS NEEDED VETERAN TOUCH

Sophomore Lamb came up with crucial shots

After all the talk about Kentucky's freshmen and one-and-dones, it took a veteran to supply the offense that allowed UK to claim NCAA title number eight.

With plucky Kansas making a run in the second half, sophomore Doron Lamb — a returning standout from UK's 2011 Final Four team — drained back-to-back three-pointers to steady Kentucky.

After the Jayhawks had come perilously close at the end of a game in which they trailed by double figures for most of the contest, it was the 6-foot-4 Queens, N.Y., product who went to the foul line with a chance to secure the national title.

There were 17.5 seconds left. The score was Kentucky 65, Kansas 59.

"I was a little nervous," Lamb said. "I just told myself to focus, take a deep breath and hope they went in."

Splash, splash.

"Fortunately, they went in," Lamb said. "And now this feels great."

Kentucky beat Kansas 67-59 Monday night to claim the 2012 NCAA Championship before 70,913 fans in the Mercedes-Benz Superdome.

It is the first NCAA crown for UK since Tubby Smith and the Comeback Cats cut down the nets in 1998. With the victory by John Calipari's third Kentucky team, UK now trails UCLA's 11 NCAA titles by three.

Much of the focus will, of course, be on UK's youth. The Cats claimed the national crown with three freshmen in the starting lineup and four among their top seven players.

But the 2012 Cats were also, in a sense, a veteran team. Lamb and fellow sophomore Terrence Jones, and senior Darius Miller, were all key components a season ago on the UK team that ended the school's post-1998 Final Four drought.

With the national title on the line, Lamb came through like a veteran.

Doron Lamb put up a shot in the first half. *Charles Bertram | Lexington Herald-Leader*

The guard hit seven of 12 shots, three of six three-pointers and five of six free throws to finish with a game-high 22 points.

After dominating much of the way, it turned out Kentucky (38-2) needed all the offense Lamb could provide.

Kansas (32-7) had only allowed two teams to shoot above 50 percent all year (UK was one of them, in a 75-65 win over the Jayhawks in November), but the Cats torched them for 53.3 percent in half one.

As a result, UK led 41-27 at halftime.

But everyone knew Kansas, which came from 13 down to beat Ohio State in the national semifinals, would make a run.

The Jayhawks made several.

Kansas pulled within 10, 48-38, with 11:55 left and had the ball. But the Jayhawks turned it over.

Lamb made them pay.

In a 35-second span, he drained a trey from the deep left corner and then another from the top of the key with 10 minutes left.

"They were huge," Kansas Coach Bill Self said. "We got it to 10 and had the ball, and we come up with nothing. (Lamb) shoots two in a row in there, gave them breathing room. It was huge in the game."

Lamb's treys restored UK's advantage to 16, 54-38, and supplied just enough room for the Cats, who wobbled down the stretch, to hold off Kansas.

Amid a bear-hugging, chest-pounding UK celebration on the Superdome Court, Lamb said Calipari told him early Monday that he was going to have a big game.

"Coach told me I was going to have a big game if I had a good shoot-around," Lamb said. "Well, my shoot-around was perfect. I just came out and tried to be aggressive and make shots."

Said Calipari: "When I watched his shoot-around, I thought he'd get 30 tonight."

The Kentucky freshmen were pretty good, too.

Anthony Davis went 1-for-10 from the floor, yet he dominated the game with six points, 16 rebounds, six blocks, five assists and three steals.

Marquis Teague drained a crucial late three-pointer and two clutch free throws and finished with 14 points. Michael Kidd-Gilchrist had 11 points and six rebounds and a crucial late-game blocked shot on Tyshawn Taylor that kept Kansas from pulling within four points with 54.6 seconds left.

BOX SCORE

KANSAS

## Player Name	TOT-FG FG-FGA	3-PT FG-FGA	FT-FTA	REBOUNDS OF	DE	TOT	PF	TP	A	TO	BLK	S	MIN
00 Robinson, Thomas.... f	6-17	0-0	6-7	5	12	17	2	18	1	1	0	0	36
05 Withey, Jeff........ c	2-8	0-0	1-1	3	4	7	2	5	1	1	4	2	32
10 Taylor, Tyshawn..... g	8-17	1-1	2-3	1	3	4	1	19	3	5	0	1	36
15 Johnson, Elijah..... g	5-13	3-7	0-0	1	1	2	1	13	2	2	0	1	36
24 Releford, Travis.... g	1-6	1-2	1-2	0	1	1	5	4	1	0	0	1	30
02 Teahan, Conner......	0-1	0-1	0-0	0	0	0	1	0	1	0	0	1	17
04 Wesley, Justin......	0-0	0-0	0-0	0	0	0	0	0	0	0	0	0	2
40 Young, Kevin........	0-0	0-0	0-2	0	3	3	4	0	0	0	1	0	11
TEAM................				1		1							
Totals..............	22-62	5-11	10-15	11	24	35	16	59	9	9	5	6	200

TOTAL FG%	1st Half:	11-33 33.3%	2nd Half:	11-29 37.9%	Game:	35.5%	DEADB
3-Pt. FG%	1st Half:	2-4 50.0%	2nd Half:	3-7 42.9%	Game:	45.5%	REBS
F Throw %	1st Half:	3-6 50.0%	2nd Half:	7-9 77.8%	Game:	66.7%	3

KENTUCKY

## Player Name	TOT-FG FG-FGA	3-PT FG-FGA	FT-FTA	REBOUNDS OF	DE	TOT	PF	TP	A	TO	BLK	S	MIN
03 Jones, Terrence..... f	4-7	0-1	1-2	1	6	7	4	9	0	2	2	1	29
23 Davis, Anthony...... f	1-10	0-0	4-6	4	12	16	2	6	5	3	6	3	36
14 Kidd-Gilchrist, M... g	4-7	0-1	3-4	2	4	6	2	11	1	1	1	0	35
20 Lamb, Doron......... g	7-12	3-6	5-6	1	1	2	2	22	3	1	0	0	35
25 Teague, Marquis..... g	5-14	2-3	2-3	1	1	2	2	14	3	2	0	0	34
01 Miller, Darius......	2-5	1-2	0-0	1	5	6	2	5	0	2	2	0	25
30 Vargas, Eloy........	0-0	0-0	0-0	0	0	0	1	0	0	0	0	0	3
33 Wiltjer, Kyle.......	0-1	0-1	0-0	0	0	0	0	0	0	0	0	0	3
TEAM................				2	2	4							
Totals..............	23-56	6-14	15-21	12	31	43	15	67	12	11	11	4	200

TOTAL FG%	1st Half:	16-30 53.3%	2nd Half:	7-26 26.9%	Game:	41.1%	DEADB
3-Pt. FG%	1st Half:	3-7 42.9%	2nd Half:	3-7 42.9%	Game:	42.9%	REBS
F Throw %	1st Half:	6-8 75.0%	2nd Half:	9-13 69.2%	Game:	71.4%	3

Officials: Verne Harris, Mark Whitehead, Mike Stuart

Technical fouls: Kansas — None. Kentucky — None.

Attendance: 70,913

Score by Periods	1st	2nd	Total
Kansas	27	32	59
Kentucky	41	26	67

Yet it was Lamb, Kentucky's often-over-looked silent assassin, who supplied the offense the Cats needed to claim title number eight.

"Man," UK's Jones said. "He hit shots, and hit big shots when we needed them."

Said Calipari: "When he's active, his motor is running, he's as good a guard as there is in college basketball."

In claiming number eight, UK's freshmen were terrific.

But it was a veteran who supplied the points needed to restore Kentucky to the top of college basketball.

Said Lamb: "This is an honor, man. It's why I came back and why we worked so hard over the summer."■

Above: Anthony Davis jumped in the arms of Michael Kidd-Gilchrist at the end of the game after defeating Kansas. *Charles Bertram | Lexington Herald-Leader*

Upper Right: Michael Kidd-Gilchrist and Terrence Jones celebrated at the end of the game after defeating Kansas in the championship game. *Mark Cornelison | Lexington Herald-Leader*

Right: John Calipari cut down the net in New Orleans. *Mark Cornelison | Lexington Herald-Leader*

SEASON RESULTS

2011-2012 SCHEDULE

Date	Opponent	Result
11/2	TRANSY (Exh.)	W, 97-53
11/7	MOREHOUSE (Exh.)	W, 125-40
11/11	MARIST	W, 108-58
11/15	Kansas	W, 75-65
11/19	Penn State	W, 85-47
11/20	Old Dominion	W, 62-52
11/23	RADFORD	W, 88-40
11/26	PORTLAND	W, 87-63
12/1	ST. JOHN'S	W, 81-59
12/3	NORTH CAROLINA	W, 73-72
12/10	at Indiana	L, 73-72
12/17	CHATTANOOGA	W, 87-62
12/20	SAMFORD	W, 82-50
12/22	LOYOLA (MD)	W, 87-63
12/28	LAMAR	W, 86-64
12/31	LOUISVILLE	W, 69-62
01/3	Arkansas-Little Rock	W, 73-51
01/7	SOUTH CAROLINA	W, 79-64
01/11	at Auburn	W, 68-53
01/14	at Tennessee	W, 65-62
01/17	ARKANSAS	W, 86-63
01/21	ALABAMA	W, 77-71
01/24	at Georgia	W, 57-44
01/28	at LSU	W, 74-50
01/31	TENNESSEE	W, 69-44
02/4	at South Carolina	W, 86-52
02/7	FLORIDA	W, 78-58
02/11	at Vanderbilt	W, 69-63
02/18	OLE MISS	W, 77-62
02/21	at Mississippi State	W, 73-64
02/25	VANDERBILT	W, 83-74
03/1	GEORGIA	W, 79-49
03/4	at Florida	W, 74-59
03/9	LSU (SEC)	W, 60-51
03/10	Florida (SEC)	W, 74-71
03/11	Vanderbilt (SEC)	L, 71-64
03/15	Western Kentucky (NCAA)	W, 81-66
03/17	Iowa State (NCAA)	W, 87-71
03/23	Indiana (NCAA)	W, 102-90
03/25	Baylor (NCAA)	W, 82-70
03/31	Louisville(NCAA)	W, 69-61
04/02	Kansas (NCAA)	W, 67-59

SEASON STATS

				TOT-FG		3-PT			
## Player Name	GP-GS	Min	Avg	FG-FGA	Pct	3FG-FGA	Pct	FT-FTA	Pct
23 Davis, Anthony.....	40-40	1281	32.0	210-337	.623	3-20	.150	144-203	.709
20 Lamb, Doron........	40-35	1249	31.2	175-369	.474	76-163	.466	123-149	.826
03 Jones, Terrence....	38-34	1114	29.3	177-354	.500	16-49	.327	99-158	.627
14 Kidd-Gilchrist, M..	40-39	1245	31.1	160-326	.491	13-51	.255	143-192	.745
25 Teague, Marquis....	40-40	1303	32.6	145-352	.412	26-80	.325	85-119	.714
01 Miller, Darius.....	40-11	1043	26.1	143-302	.474	56-149	.376	55-69	.797
33 Wiltjer, Kyle......	40-0	462	11.6	71-162	.438	35-81	.432	22-27	.815
13 Malone, Sam........	6-0	13	2.2	3-6	.500	0-0	.000	0-0	.000
30 Vargas, Eloy.......	33-1	198	6.0	12-36	.333	0-1	.000	4-13	.308
32 Long, Brian........	12-0	17	1.4	0-1	.000	0-0	.000	2-4	.500
05 Polson, Jarrod.....	11-0	31	2.8	0-2	.000	0-1	.000	1-4	.250
10 Beckham, Twany.....	16-0	44	2.8	0-1	.000	0-0	.000	0-0	.000
Total.............	40	8000		1096-2248	.488	225-595	.378	678-938	.723
Opponents..........	40	8000		889-2379	.374	219-689	.318	426-614	.694

	REBOUNDS											
## Player Name	Off	Def	Tot	Avg	PF	FO	A	TO	Blk	Stl	Pts	Avg
23 Davis, Anthony.....	119	296	415	10.4	78	1	50	41	186	54	567	14.2
20 Lamb, Doron........	15	93	108	2.7	72	0	60	44	2	19	549	13.7
03 Jones, Terrence....	96	176	272	7.2	91	3	51	62	68	49	469	12.3
14 Kidd-Gilchrist, M..	103	194	297	7.4	97	5	75	87	37	39	476	11.9
25 Teague, Marquis....	17	84	101	2.5	91	1	191	109	11	37	401	10.0
01 Miller, Darius.....	36	74	110	2.8	87	0	82	58	13	33	397	9.9
33 Wiltjer, Kyle......	26	44	70	1.8	44	0	16	27	17	5	199	5.0
13 Malone, Sam........	0	2	2	0.3	0	0	1	4	0	0	6	1.0
30 Vargas, Eloy.......	20	36	56	1.7	26	0	2	6	10	3	28	0.8
32 Long, Brian........	1	1	2	0.2	0	0	0	0	0	0	2	0.2
05 Polson, Jarrod.....	0	4	4	0.4	4	0	1	5	0	2	1	0.1
10 Beckham, Twany.....	2	6	8	0.5	0	0	2	1	0	1	0	0.0
TEAM..............	52	59	111	2.8	3		9				0	
Total.............	487	1069	1556	38.9	593	10	531	453	344	242	3095	77.4
Opponents..........	487	799	1286	32.2	750	-	420	466	133	218	2423	60.6

RECORD:	OVERALL	HOME	AWAY	NEUTRAL
ALL GAMES...........	(38-2)	(18-0)	(8-1)	(12-1)
CONFERENCE..........	(16-0)	(8-0)	(8-0)	(0-0)
NON-CONFERENCE......	(22-2)	(10-0)	(0-1)	(12-1)

Score by Periods	1st	2nd	Total
Kentucky.....................	1511	1584	3095
Opponents.....................	1139	1284	2423

Deadball Rebounds:	OFF	DEF	TOTAL
Kentucky.....................	109	24	133
Opponents.....................	98	17	115

Anthony Davis hugged coach John Calipari after defeating Kansas. *Charles Bertram | Lexington Herald-Leader*